GOOD
Arguments

GOOD
Arguments

MAKING YOUR CASE
IN WRITING AND PUBLIC SPEAKING

RICHARD A. HOLLAND JR.
AND BENJAMIN K. FORREST

B
Baker Academic
a division of Baker Publishing Group
Grand Rapids, Michigan

Published by Baker Academic
a division of Baker Publishing Group
P.O. Box 6287, Grand Rapids, MI 49516-6287
www.bakeracademic.com

Printed in the United States of America

Library of Congress Cataloging-in-Publication Data
Names: Holland, Richard A., Jr., author. | Forrest, Benjamin K., author.
Title: Good arguments : making your case in writing and public speaking / Richard A.
    Holland, Jr. and Benjamin K. Forrest.
Description: Grand Rapids, MI : Baker Academic, a division of Baker Publishing
    Group, [2017]
Identifiers: LCCN 2017000743 | ISBN 9780801097799 (pbk.)
Subjects: LCSH: Reasoning. | Logic.
Classification: LCC BC177 .H645 2017 | DDC 168—dc23
LC record available at https://lccn.loc.gov/2017000743

17 18 19 20 21 22 23   7 6 5 4 3 2 1

To Larissa,
for your unending patience and love.

RAH

To Reagan, Hudson, and Graham,
with prayers that you spend your life sharing Christ
through your actions, love, and arguments.

BKF

CONTENTS

ACKNOWLEDGMENTS

As with any project, there are many individuals behind the scenes who helped bring this book to fruition. We would first like to thank the entire Baker Academic team, especially R. David Nelson, David Cramer, Steve Ayers, Jeremy Wells, and freelance editor Ryan Davis. Their encouragement gave us the ability to take on this project and see it through to completion. In addition we would like to thank Christopher P. Davis, Ronnie Campbell, Christopher Bosson, and Josh Erb for feedback on the case studies. Their insight and critique were helpful and encouraging.

Rich would like to thank his wife, Larissa, for her loyalty and encouragement. He also wishes to thank his dear friends Daphne and Gene Woodall for providing their home as a writing retreat, for their constant love and encouragement, and for being family.

Ben would like to thank his wife, Lerisa, for her constant encouragement and for listening to the formation and planning of this text with patience and interest. Her constant encouragement is a blessing and a gift!

Lastly, we would like to thank the Lord for calling us to know him and share him with the world. We pray that our experiences can be invested into the body for the equipping of the saints for the work of the ministry unto God's glory.

INTRODUCTION

Why Arguments Are Good

Argument is a word that is easily misunderstood. For many of us, hearing this word brings to mind something unpleasant or something we try to avoid. When a friend comes to you saying that she has recently been in an argument with an acquaintance, this is typically bad news. It involves dispute, conflict, disagreement, heightened emotions, and stress. This may be your initial reaction if you are reading this book as an assignment for a class. Thankfully, this book is not about verbal disputes, fights, emotional disagreements, or shouting matches. The word *argument*, as we are using it, simply refers to the process of giving reasons or evidence in support of a belief or claim. An argument is a series of statements: a claim and one or more additional statements given as reasons that we should think the claim is true. The main claim being made is usually called the *conclusion* (even though the conclusion often comes at the beginning of an argument, rather than at the end). Each statement that supports the conclusion is called a *premise*. While no set number of premises is required in an argument, there must be at least one. So, at a minimum, an argument is composed of at least two statements: the conclusion and at least one premise that supports the conclusion.

One can hardly pick up a textbook introducing philosophy or logic without hearing about the ancient Greek philosopher named

Socrates. These books often use Socrates in demonstrating what an argument looks like, as follows:

> All men are mortal.
> Socrates is a man.
> Therefore, Socrates is mortal.

The first two statements are the premises of this particular argument; they are given as evidence supporting the truth of the last statement. The last statement is the conclusion. Of course, when the statements are arranged and presented in this form, it is easy to identify the premises and the conclusion, but in everyday conversation, people rarely make their premises and conclusion this clear. Instead, someone might say, "Socrates is mortal. After all, he is only a man!" When the statements are arranged in this way, it might be more difficult for you to identify the premises and the conclusion, but it is an argument nonetheless.

An argument is not a fight or dispute; it is a presentation of reasons that support a belief or claim.

You might be surprised to learn that even the Bible makes use of arguments. Consider this familiar story from Matthew 12:9–14:

> [Jesus] went on from there and entered their synagogue. And a man was there with a withered hand. And they asked him, "Is it lawful to heal on the Sabbath?"—so that they might accuse him. He said to them, "Which one of you who has a sheep, if it falls into a pit on the Sabbath, will not take hold of it and lift it out? Of how much more value is a man than a sheep! So it is lawful to do good on the Sabbath." Then he said to the man, "Stretch out your hand." And the man stretched it out, and it was restored, healthy like the other. But the Pharisees went out and conspired against him, how to destroy him.

In this encounter between Jesus and his detractors, Jesus gives an argument in response to the question from the Pharisees. The main points of his argument can be summarized as follows:

It is lawful to help a sheep out of a pit on the Sabbath.

A man is much more valuable than a sheep.

Therefore, it is lawful to heal a man on the Sabbath.[1]

The Pharisees asked Jesus the simple question: "Is it lawful to heal on the Sabbath?" Jesus's answer is obviously yes. But Jesus doesn't simply answer the question. Instead, he presents an argument: he makes a claim and gives a logical, systematic account of the reasoning that supports his claim.

It is not very common to discuss reason and argument in the context of what are normally considered matters of faith. Sometimes those in Christian circles view belief and acceptance as good, virtuous responses to the things of God, while argument and reason are either bad responses or merely tools of those who lack faith. But this shouldn't be the case. God created us as rational creatures; the laws of logic and the rules of good reasoning are what they are because of who God is. Human reason, though imperfect and fallen, is nevertheless something that is very good and God-ordained. Human reason has God as its author, and perhaps this is why the Bible contains so many appeals to reason. Since God endowed humans with reasoning capabilities, we are stewards of our reasoning abilities. God expects us to *reason well*, and presenting good arguments that support our beliefs is one way to do that. When we reason well and present good arguments, we reflect God's character.

> When we reason well and present good arguments, we reflect God's character.

In addition to the fact that presenting good arguments honors God, another important motivation for providing reasons that support your beliefs is that you want to persuade your audience. In other words, you think your claim is true, so you want your audience to believe it as well. Dubious speakers will often use sophisticated rhetoric in order to trick someone into agreeing to something, but in these cases the audience almost always recants later and rejects what the speaker offered. Instead of tricking someone, the goal of a good argument

1. For a detailed discussion of this example and its hidden premises, with extended examination of logic in the Bible, see L. Russ Bush, *A Handbook for Christian Philosophy* (Grand Rapids: Zondervan, 1991), 56–66.

should be to persuade someone to adopt the new belief *because they believe it*, not because they were mesmerized by rhetorical skill. Those who craft good arguments want their audience not just to grant superficial agreement with the claim being made but to "own it" and adopt it as their own. When you think of it this way, you can probably see that presenting arguments is essential for effective communication about the most important things in life.

> People actually expect us to present good arguments. Doing so is a way to show them the respect they deserve.

When you want to persuade your audience, you will be motivated to present good arguments. In many cases your audience will want you to present good arguments as well. Indeed, it is obvious from everyday conversation that people actually *expect* us to present arguments as a matter of routine. When someone asks you, "How do you know *that*?" or "Why *should* I?" or "What makes you think it is *true*?" they expect you to clearly articulate—in a logical and systematic way—the basis of your claim of knowledge, the reasons they should do something, or the evidence you have that indicates something is true. In other words, they expect you to provide a good argument. You must remember that the members of your audience—people made in the image of God— have the same reasoning abilities that you do. Because they intuitively understand the basic principles of reasoning and logic, you owe it to them to present good arguments, and doing so is a way to show them the respect they deserve.

Because people expect arguments, there are many situations in various contexts in which the best thing you can do is present a good argument. One obvious situation is preaching. Delivering a sermon is the kind of task that calls for good arguments. The preacher will no doubt call on listeners to believe something or do something (or both). Quite naturally, then, it makes sense for the preacher to clearly articulate, in a systematic way, the reasons why listeners should adopt the belief or take the action they are called to take. Some people hold many negative connotations about preachers and sermons. This negativity does not arise from preachers presenting arguments; it arises from preachers *not* presenting *good* arguments. If the preacher simply tells listeners what to do or believe without giving good reasons or evidence or supporting claims with logical, rational support, the listeners are not likely to respond as the preacher may have hoped.

Engaging in apologetics is another situation in which arguments are essential. Apologetics is the practice of defending a particular position, belief, or viewpoint, and such a defense will almost always need arguments if it is going to be successful. If someone has presented a challenge and suggested that Christianity is irrational, Christians must present a rational argument—or a series of arguments—in response to that challenge that clearly demonstrates the logic, reasoning, and evidence supporting Christian belief. And when the apologist is not busy responding to challenges, she will certainly want to develop other positive arguments for Christianity that can stand on their own and serve to demonstrate that Christianity is true, reasonable, or rational.

Beyond these, countless situations arise in which presenting a good argument is the best thing you can do. In the course of everyday life, when someone asks why you voted for one candidate and not the other, why you believe in God, or why you took a particular course of action, you should be able to answer with a well-reasoned argument. Real answers to these kinds of questions call for you to give clear, logical support for your position, which means you will need to develop and present arguments. Sometimes the questions asked or the issues addressed are complex enough that extended arguments are necessary. In situations like this, many shorter arguments can work together to make a larger case. Like the various small mechanisms that fit together to make one machine, many short arguments can work together to form one extended argument.

Being able to develop and employ successful arguments is a skill that can provide many benefits. As suggested above, arguments can help you defend your beliefs against challenges to them, and arguments can help you persuade others to adopt a belief, accept a conclusion, or take a particular course of action. Being able to develop good arguments can also result in great personal benefit. When you are not quite sure what you believe,

> There are countless situations in which presenting a good argument is the best thing you can do.

thinking in terms of an argument can help clarify your belief. This will also help define (for yourself and for others) precisely why you believe what you believe. Making good arguments can increase your confidence in your beliefs because arguments enable you to think carefully about the good reasons supporting your beliefs. When you are confronted with a new claim and want to know whether you should believe that it is true, developing an argument can help you think carefully about the claim and decide to accept or reject it. Developing an argument is also helpful when you want to take the right course of action. It can help you rule out competing alternatives and decide on the best way forward. All of these reasons for understanding and employing good arguments motivated us to write this book.

In the chapters that follow, you will find a series of explanations and guidelines designed to help you understand what goes into making good arguments. You will also find some practical tips and some warnings about potential pitfalls. It is our hope that after reading this book you will understand how arguments can be good and know how to develop good arguments of your own.

1

The Basics of Good Arguments

People often have a misconception about arguments. The arguments of everyday conversation are quite different from what we have in mind for this book. When Ben was a doctoral student engaged to his wonderful wife-to-be, Lerisa, he had one of those classic arguments that often take place as two people prepare for marriage. They were sitting in a parking lot arguing, and the more they argued, the louder Ben's voice grew. As his voice rose, Lerisa looked at him and said, "Arguments aren't about winning!" It stopped him in the middle of his sentence—not because he suddenly agreed with her side of the argument but because what she said went against everything he believed based on his experience. Growing up in an opinionated family, Ben was conditioned to think that arguing was about winning and that the loudest person always won. What Lerisa revealed to Ben that day stood in sharp contrast to everything he knew about arguing. She pointed out that an argument is not a battle to be fought and won but rather a means for communicating a message.

Rich's family background is similar. He also grew up in the context of a family dynamic in which the loudest, most forceful person "won" the argument. Perhaps your experience is similar and you too have ingrained in your thinking the idea that arguments are like battles to be fought and won, and the loudest, most aggressive combatants win.

Perhaps because of experiences like this, you now recoil at the thought of engaging in an argument.

> An argument is the process of giving a systematic account of reasons in support of a claim or belief.

It is vital to understand that the conception of argumentation we just described is a misconception. Some people do indeed argue that way, but that isn't what an argument is all about. Our definition of an argument is *the process of giving a systematic account of reasons in support of a claim or belief.* Instead of thinking about "winning" an argument, we would do better to think about "winning someone over to our side"—that is, we want to persuade someone that the position we are defending really is true, to convince them so that they genuinely change their mind and come to agree with the position we are defending. We aim to persuade, encourage, and prepare, not to win. And if we can't thoroughly convince someone that our position is true, we can, at the very least, use effective argumentation to defend our position as a reasonable option among various choices. An argument should never be a shouting match, and the loudest participant doesn't automatically win. In fact, if our main goal is to bring about genuine persuasion, then shouting is the least likely tactic to bring about this goal. Instead, skillful arguers will learn to give clear, straightforward, easy-to-understand reasons that support a claim, without getting into a rhetorical competition or shouting match.

Claims and Beliefs

As we consider this perspective on what an argument is, we must recognize at the outset that claims and beliefs go hand in hand. For anything you believe, you can state that belief in the form of a claim. For example, you may believe that a portion of the film *The Hunger Games* was filmed in North Carolina. It is easy to recognize that belief when you communicate it in the form of a claim. If you are sitting with friends watching the film, you may say something like, "Part of this movie was filmed in North Carolina." This statement is a claim and communicates what you believe—in this case, what you believe about *The Hunger Games* being filmed (in part) in North Carolina. We'll return to the concept of beliefs in a later chapter; for now it is sufficient to recognize that when we communicate our beliefs to others, we state them in the form of claims. So for most of our discussion, we will use the words *claim* and *belief* interchangeably.

Stating a claim by itself is almost never good enough if we want others to understand why we believe what we believe, or if we want to persuade them that we have good reasons supporting our beliefs. Considering the example above, in some contexts it will probably be insufficient to simply make the claim about where *The Hunger Games* was filmed. Instead of merely stating the claim, we must provide good reasons that help show why we think that claim is true. Sometimes claims don't need much in the way of supporting reasons. If you are watching *The Hunger Games* with a group of friends who don't think your claim is all that important, they might just accept it without any supporting reasons, so you probably don't need to say much else. This is similar to many everyday claims we make. For example, a claim like "It's raining" doesn't need much of an argument for support. We can just point out the window and say, "Look! It's raining." But for complicated or contentious claims, or claims made to an audience that is inclined to disagree, an argument is needed to justify and support the claim. The more contentious or divisive the claim, the more careful, well-thought-out, and intentional the argument must be. We don't need to support unimportant or uninteresting claims with good arguments, but for the important questions of life—such as questions about the morality of capital punishment, the existence of God, and the nature of marriage—being able to argue well becomes an indispensable skill. Claims about important questions will always require good arguments to support them.

> Arguments are beneficial not just for others but for yourself as well; they help you communicate and support your personal beliefs.

Essential Features of a Good Argument

Good arguments are necessary not just for supporting your claims for the benefit of those who are reading or listening to your argument; they are also important as you begin grappling with your own beliefs. In order to argue well, you must first learn how to develop good arguments by yourself, independent of a discussion with someone else; and if you are able to present a rational defense of a claim palatable enough to quench your own skepticism, it is likely that you will be able to present it to others for their edification as well.

But what makes a *good* argument? At this point it is tempting for us to present an extended discussion of bad arguments and the bad reasoning that goes along with them—because bad reasoning is so common and is often disguised as good reasoning—but we'll save that for a later chapter. In the remainder of this chapter, we focus on the essential features of good arguments. This is because good reasoning will form the fundamental building blocks of good arguments.

In this book's introduction, we briefly described the basic components of a short argument: an argument contains a series of statements (*premises*) that are intended to support another statement (the *conclusion*). An argument's conclusion is the claim or belief that is being defended or supported by the premises, and the premises are the reasons that attempt to prove that the claim is true. When arguments are written out formally (as they might appear in textbooks on logic), they start by giving the premises and end by stating the conclusion. Written out in sequence, an argument might appear like this:

> **An argument's conclusion is the claim or belief that is being defended or supported by the premises.**

Premise (Reason) 1

Premise (Reason) 2

∴ Conclusion (i.e., the claim or belief that is being defended by these two premises)[1]

---

1. The ∴ sign is used in logic and mathematics and means *therefore*, indicating that a conclusion is being drawn.

However, when arguments are written in ordinary prose or stated orally, they don't always proceed in such a linear order. Sometimes the conclusion is stated first, and sometimes it is stated in the middle of the premises, so it can be difficult to identify the various parts. When arguments are long and complex, it can be even more difficult to identify the parts and see how they fit together. Long arguments often contain arguments inside other arguments, which further complicates the situation. But no matter how short or long, and no matter what order the various items are presented in, all arguments share the same basic components: claims and reasons that support those claims.

Good Arguments State Clearly All of Their Essential Elements

As we have said, when short arguments are written formally, they often begin with premises and end with the conclusion. Recall the famous example we mentioned in the introduction:

All men are mortal. (Premise)
Socrates is a man. (Premise)
Therefore, Socrates is mortal. (Conclusion)

Writing arguments in this form can indeed be quite helpful when we are engaged in analyzing an argument that someone else has given. That is why introductory textbooks on philosophy and logic are full of example arguments written out just like this. In most cases the purpose is to help the student identify the key parts of the arguments and to differentiate good arguments from bad ones. However, many arguments—indeed most arguments—that we encounter are presented outside the context of the logic textbook. They might be given orally as a part of a public policy speech or a sermon. Or they might be written in ordinary prose in newspaper articles, journals, academic papers, or blog entries. In these varied contexts, it is rather uncommon to have a simple, short argument written out like the one above about Socrates, with two or three premises leading to a simple conclusion. For each argument we encounter, what really matters is whether the essential elements in the argument are stated clearly. No matter the form or the context in which they are presented, good arguments will always clearly state their claims and all relevant supporting reasons. As you learn to develop your own arguments, one of the most important skills to develop is the skill of clearly stating every element that is important to the argument.

Some arguments do not state their premises clearly; this is a characteristic of weak arguments that cannot do what they are intended to do. Premises are designed to be declarative statements that convey some meaningful fact in support of the claim. Sometimes, however, a meaningful fact essential to the argument is not stated at all. Such unstated elements are called *hidden premises*. Consider again our example argument about Socrates. Someone might put it this way: "Socrates is mortal. After all, he is only a man!" When the argument is stated this way, there is one hidden premise: *All men are mortal*. Many people will be able to grasp this premise intuitively, so the fact that it is hidden in this particular argument may not do too much harm. However, when a hidden premise is controversial, or when the audience is simply ignorant of the hidden premise, the argument is likely to fail at its intended mission of supporting the claim or persuading the audience. Consider this one: "Of course God exists. Just look at the wonderfully intricate beauty in nature." In this example, there are several hidden premises, most of which are likely to be controversial or unknown to an audience who does not already believe the claim "God exists." Some of the hidden premises might be:

- Intricate beauty is objective and recognizable.
- Intricate beauty indicates design.
- Design requires a designer.
- Given the extent of the intricate beauty in nature, the designer must be very powerful.

Hopefully you can see these aren't the only hidden premises essential to this example argument. Many other premises would need to be stated for this kind of argument to get off the ground. Moreover, most of the hidden premises in this case are so controversial that each would require a persuasive argument of its own for support, which means that almost no one in an objective audience would think that this example argument is good enough when several premises remain unstated and unsupported. Obvious or uncontroversial hidden premises might not make too much of a difference, but failing to state essential premises that are controversial or not obvious to your audience makes for a weak argument. A good argument will not have this weakness. A good argument will clearly state each premise that supports the claim and will not let any other essential premise remain hidden.

While some arguments have hidden premises, other arguments fail to clearly state the main claim. Having a hidden claim is probably a bit rarer than having a hidden premise, but it does happen. Consider this example: Perhaps you have overheard a conversation between friends in response to one friend harming the other or committing some fault against the other. The one who is in the wrong might say, "Well, I'm only human!" It might not look like it at first, but this is a kind of argument. The person who says this is asserting that the other person ought to forgive the wrong that has been committed. This is the main claim that went unstated: "You ought to forgive this wrong that I have committed." So the argument "I'm only human!" is a weak argument, mainly because the main claim is unstated. Of course there are also at least two hidden premises: "all humans commit these kinds of wrongs" and "one ought to forgive faults that are common to all humans." Good arguments state the main claim clearly, along with all the essential supporting premises. This should be a fairly easy task to accomplish because, when making an argument, we are all aware of our beliefs and claims. Therefore, stating our beliefs and claims clearly is the easiest part of making a good argument.

Good Arguments State the Claim Up Front

Another factor to consider is the location of the main claim in the argument—the where and how of stating the claim. Put simply, good arguments state their claim up front, before supporting reasons are given. As we pointed out above, when short arguments are written out formally (as they appear in an introductory logic textbook), they typically state the claim last, as the conclusion. In the context of the logic textbook, the order of elements in the argument is almost always presented solely for the purpose of analyzing the argument. Presenting the premises first and the conclusion last is a convenient way to help students understand what goes into an argument and how to properly identify all the parts. However, when it comes to actually crafting and delivering a good argument to an audience you want to persuade, this linear order is almost always unhelpful. Instead, stating the main claim at the start is more likely to bring about the desired result. In the course of normal conversation, presenting an effective short argument might go something like this:

> Me: Socrates is mortal.
> You: Oh, really? How do we know that?
> Me: Well, Socrates is a man, right?
> You: Sure.
> Me: And all men are mortal, aren't they?
> You: Yes.
> Me: Well if Socrates is a man and all men are mortal, Socrates must be mortal.
> You: Oh! I see! Yes, you are right.

Stating the main claim at the very beginning sets the context so that the audience knows where you are headed and understands why the supporting premises are given and how they are connected to the claim. If the claim is not stated clearly at the beginning, the audience is likely to be confused. Imagine if the first part of the argument given was "All men are mortal." In that case the audience might assume that this is your main point and miss the fact that you are really trying to prove that Socrates is mortal. Consider this alternative discussion:

> Me: All men are mortal.
> You: Probably, but how would we know?
> Me: Hold on a second, let me finish. Socrates was a man.
> You: Who?
> Me: Socrates. He was a man.

You: Wasn't he a great philosopher? And what does that have to do with our mortality?

Me: You are missing my point! I'm trying to show you that Socrates is mortal.

You: Well, why didn't you just say so?

Good arguments eliminate this possible confusion by clearly stating the main claim up front before the supporting ideas are offered.

Stating the claim at the very beginning of an argument is especially important for long arguments. We will return to this in a later chapter, but for now it is important to mention two common contexts for making a long, extended argument: the academic research paper and the speech or sermon. In an academic context, the research paper is a work of scholarship in which the author (typically a student) advances an original thesis and supports that thesis with good arguments. The *thesis* is just the main claim that the author wants to make, and the entire paper is a series of connected arguments that are intended to support the claim (to persuade the reader that the thesis is true). To say it another way, the thesis is the *conclusion* of the argument. Too often students who do not know how to make good arguments do not even mention the thesis until the conclusion paragraph of the paper. Unfortunately, this means that the professor will have to read the entire paper to know what the main point is and then will need to read it again to evaluate whether the arguments presented adequately support the thesis. Here is a paper writer's rule of thumb: don't save the conclusion for the conclusion! A good research paper (like any good argument) will always state the thesis up front—in the introduction to the paper—so that the professor (or any other reader) knows where the paper is going. The same holds true for a speech or sermon. Your audience will appreciate your argument if you clearly state at the outset what belief you are defending or what claim you are attempting to demonstrate is true. It gives your listener the context necessary to follow and understand your argument, which means your argument is more likely to be successful.

> Don't save the conclusion for the conclusion!

Good Arguments Properly Connect Premises to the Claim

Good arguments require good premises—premises that appropriately support the main claim of the argument and can therefore help persuade an audience that the claim is true. There are two ways that a premise can fail to support the claim well: (1) the premise is false, or (2) the premise does not adequately support the conclusion. Obviously, a false premise can never do a good job supporting the main claim of an argument, but perhaps you haven't given much consideration to how a true premise is connected to the claim and whether that connection provides adequate support. Consider this example:

> Capital punishment is immoral. Studies show that a shockingly high number of those convicted of capital offenses are actually innocent. Moreover, a disproportionate number of minorities are sentenced to death, indicating racial bias in the court system and possibly in policing policies and tactics.

In this example the main claim is that capital punishment is immoral. Two premises are offered to support this claim: a high number of convicts are actually innocent, and a disproportionate number of minorities are sentenced to death. Let's just say for the sake of discussion that those two premises are true. Even though these premises are true, they still do not do a good job in supporting the main claim because they are not properly connected to it. Whether some convicts are innocent and whether minorities are disproportionately sentenced to death are not directly relevant to the question of whether capital punishment itself is immoral. These premises can support other kinds of claims, such as claims about the need to reform the civil justice system in the United States or about racial inequality. But if we want to support the claim that capital punishment itself is immoral, we will need to offer premises that are related to how we determine whether capital punishment is moral or immoral.

Arguments like the example above aren't good arguments because they make mistakes in reasoning. In the example, the argument's mistake is in presenting premises that are not relevant to the conclusion (and therefore cannot possibly support the claim). Good arguments do not make this kind of mistake in reasoning. In some cases it might *appear* as if the premise supports the claim, and this calls for careful evaluation of the argument and of whether the premises are relevant. A special term is used to describe good arguments, arguments in which the premises are properly connected to the conclusion. We say that such arguments are *valid* arguments. When arguments are valid, the premises are relevant to the conclusion and actually give us good reasons to think that the conclusion is true. Sometimes people use the word *valid* to describe something that is true, but it is important to recognize that when we are analyzing arguments, we do not use the word *valid* as a synonym for *true*. A valid argument is simply one that does not make a mistake in reasoning, and therefore the premises are properly connected to the main claim. In fact, an argument can still be valid even if it has false premises and a false conclusion. To say an argument is valid is not to say that it is true. Rather, to say an argument is valid is to say that *if* the premises are true, they constitute good reasons to think that the conclusion is true because they are properly connected to the conclusion. A valid argument is one that does not make any mistakes in reasoning.

> The word fallacy or fallacious never means "false."

A bad argument, on the other hand, does contain a mistake in reasoning (or perhaps many mistakes in reasoning). *Fallacy* is the word logicians use to refer to a mistake in reasoning, and an argument that contains one or more fallacies is called a *fallacious* argument. Whether the premises of a fallacious argument are true or false, they do not constitute good grounds for thinking that the conclusion is true because they do not have the proper logical relationship to the conclusion. Sometimes people will use the word *fallacy* to describe something that is false. However, in the analysis of arguments, the word *fallacy* or *fallacious* never means false. In fact, a fallacious argument can have all true premises and a true conclusion. The reason for this is simply that *fallacy* is only intended to point out a logical mistake in reasoning. Consider this example:

> I'm sure that God exists. After all, the vast majority of the people in the world believe in God.

The claim being made in this argument is that God exists, and the premise being offered is that most people believe in God. Let's assume for the sake of discussion that both the main claim (God exists) and the supporting premise (most people believe in God) are indeed true. Even though every element in the argument is true, this is still a fallacious argument. No matter how popular it is to believe in God, this can't help us determine whether God actually exists (as if God's existence depends on a popularity contest). To say that an argument is fallacious is not to say that any part of it is false. Instead, it is simply to say that the premises of the argument do not have the proper relationship to the conclusion—that it makes some kind of mistake in reasoning. We will return to the discussion of fallacies in a later chapter. There we will describe some of the more common fallacies that appear in arguments, show why they are fallacies, and give some tips on how to avoid them. Hopefully this process will help you learn the skill of properly connecting the premises in your argument to the claim you want to make so that you can avoid the more common mistakes in reasoning. Meanwhile, it is sufficient to recognize that fallacious arguments are those that make mistakes in reasoning (their premises are not properly connected to their main claims), and valid arguments are those that do not make mistakes in reasoning.

> Fallacious arguments are those that make mistakes in reasoning; valid arguments are those that do not make mistakes in reasoning.

Conclusion

This chapter has laid the foundations for the remainder of the book. We have defined the two main parts of an argument: the main claim (which is called the *conclusion* of an argument) and the reasons that support the conclusion (called the *premises*). We pointed out that good arguments will always state their premises and claims clearly, and they will almost always state the main claim at the beginning of the argument so that the audience knows where the argument is headed. We also highlighted the importance of having premises that are properly connected to the claim. We pointed out that valid arguments have premises that are properly connected to the claim, while fallacious arguments do not. In the next chapter we will explore two kinds of reasoning, inductive and deductive, and we will give a brief overview of what are sometimes called "the laws of logic."

2

Reasoning and Logic

In the previous chapter we discussed the features of good arguments. After briefly discussing the definition of an argument and the connection between beliefs and claims, we mentioned foundational principles for crafting a good argument:

- State clearly all of the essential elements in the argument.
- State the main claim up front.
- Make sure all premises are properly connected to the main claim.

In this chapter we begin by describing the two basic kinds of good arguments, and then we devote some discussion to logic.

Two Kinds of Good Reasoning: Deductive and Inductive

Previously we explained the importance of an argument having premises that are properly connected to the claim being made. The skill that we employ to make these proper connections is the skill of *reasoning*. If we want to craft a good argument, we must use good reasoning skills to present premises that are properly related to the claim we are making. There are two basic types of good reasoning: deductive and inductive. Using good deductive reasoning helps us to create good deductive arguments. Using good inductive reasoning helps us to create good inductive arguments.

Deductive Arguments

Deductive arguments employ deductive reasoning to present premises that support the conclusion.[1] The simplest way to describe deductive reasoning is to say that a good argument using deductive reasoning leads to a conclusion that cannot possibly be false, assuming that all the premises are true. In the study of reasoning and argument, *valid* is the term used to describe a good deductive argument. As we mentioned in the previous chapter, in everyday language people will sometimes use the word *valid* to mean *true*. This is not how we use it here. To say that an argument is *valid* simply means that the premises are properly connected to the conclusion. A valid deductive argument is one in which, if the premises are true, the conclusion is certainly true. The argument about Socrates that we have repeated several times is an example of a valid deductive argument. Here it is again:

> All men are mortal. (Premise)
> Socrates is a man. (Premise)
> Therefore, Socrates is mortal. (Conclusion)

One key feature of valid deductive argumentation should be noted at this point: in a valid deductive argument, everything about the conclusion is already stated in the premises. In other words, the conclusion to a valid deductive argument does not add any new information; it is simply the natural consequence of the premises being true. Once we grasp the idea that all men are mortal and that Socrates is a man, we need not add any new information at all to understand that Socrates

A good argument using deductive reasoning leads to a conclusion that cannot possibly be false, assuming that all the premises are true.

---

1. Recall that the *conclusion* to an argument is the main claim that is being supported, and it is stated up front at the beginning of a good argument.

is mortal. The conclusion is certain, and all the information we need is stated in the premises.

Here is another example of a valid deductive argument, this one about presidential elections:

> If George W. Bush was elected in the 2000 presidential election, he would be the forty-third president of the United States.
>
> George W. Bush was elected president in the 2000 election.
>
> Therefore, George W. Bush became the forty-third president of the United States.

This is a *valid* deductive argument. The two premises are properly connected to the conclusion, and they contain all the information we need in order to know that if the premises are true, the conclusion is certainly true. In this example, since both premises are true, we know for certain that the conclusion is true. This is what deductive arguments look like: as long as the argument is valid and the premises are true, the conclusion is certainly true. There is, quite literally, no doubt about it.

Unfortunately, valid deductive arguments often contain false premises. It is important to emphasize again that *valid* does not mean *true*. Valid arguments are those whose premises are properly connected to the conclusion, whether they are true or false. Here is an example:

> All past presidents of the United States were born before 1941.
>
> Bill Clinton was president of the United States.
>
> Therefore, Bill Clinton was born before 1941.

This too is a valid deductive argument. The two premises are properly connected to the conclusion—that is, they contain all the information we need to know that, if they are true, the conclusion is certainly true. But let's say we also happen to know that George W. Bush (a past president) was born in 1946. This information tells us that the first premise of this argument must be false. Since that premise is false, it cannot help us establish the conclusion. So while we can be sure that the conclusion of a valid deductive argument is true *if* the premises are true, the fact that some premises may be false leaves room for doubt about the conclusion, even when the argument's form is valid.

Some valid deductive arguments contain false premises *and a false conclusion*. The argument about Bill Clinton is a good example of this because Bill Clinton was born in 1946. Here is another example—this one from the New Testament:

Nothing good can come from Nazareth.

Jesus came from Nazareth.

Therefore, Jesus is not good.[2]

Again, this is a *valid* argument: if the premises are true, then the conclusion is certainly true. However, this argument has one true premise, one false premise, and a false conclusion. It is true that Jesus grew up in Nazareth, so premise 2 is true. However, we have other well-established reasons to think that the conclusion is false. Jesus's goodness is perhaps one of the least-debated facts in all of human history. If we know that Jesus is good, then this alone is reason to reject the first premise. But we probably wouldn't have to work too hard to come up with another example of something good that came out of Nazareth. So even though this argument is valid, it has one false premise and a false conclusion.

Some valid deductive arguments contain one or more false premises, but unlike the previous two examples, they still have true conclusions. Consider this example:

The capital of Pennsylvania is the home of the Pittsburgh Steelers.

Pittsburgh is the capital of Pennsylvania.

Therefore, Pittsburgh is the home of the Pittsburgh Steelers.

This is a valid deductive argument. The premises offered contain all the information necessary to lead to a certain conclusion. If the two premises are true, then the conclusion is certainly true. But, as we hope you already know, both premises are actually false. Harrisburg, not Pittsburgh, is the capital of Pennsylvania, and the capital

2. Adapted from John 1:46. The rhetorical question Nathanael asked was "Can anything good come out of Nazareth?" The implied answer, of course, is no.

of Pennsylvania is not the home of the Pittsburgh Steelers. But the conclusion is indeed true: Pittsburgh is the home of the Pittsburgh Steelers. So this is an example of a valid deductive argument with two false premises and a true conclusion.

So far we have provided examples of valid deductive arguments with true premises and a true conclusion, with false premises and a false conclusion, and with false premises and a true conclusion. However, a valid deductive argument can never have true premises and a false conclusion. This is part of what it means to be a valid deductive argument: if the premises are true, then the conclusion is certainly true. If we already know that the conclusion of the argument is false and that the premises are true, then we know that it can't be a valid argument.[3]

"If . . . Then" Deductive Syllogisms

A syllogism is a particular kind of deductive argument that has two premises and a conclusion; each of the two premises share a common term that isn't in the conclusion. While there are many particular kinds, or *forms*, of syllogisms, two of them are so common that it is worth describing them here. Once you learn their basic structure and how to recognize them, you will probably begin to see them in all kinds of arguments and perhaps even in your own thinking. These two forms both make use of "if . . . then" statements. In each of the following two argument forms, we use two letters, A and B, to stand for any two content statements. It doesn't really matter what they are because we are just looking at the form of the arguments, not the particular content. The two forms are referred to by their Latin names, *modus ponens* and *modus tollens*.

Form of Argument	*Modus Ponens*	*Modus Tollens*
Premise 1	If A, then B	If A, then B
Premise 2	A	Not B
Conclusion	Therefore, B	Therefore, not A

3. Arguments that aren't valid are called *fallacious* because they contain one or more fallacies. They make some mistake in reasoning, such that the premises are not properly connected to the conclusion. We will discuss fallacies in a later chapter.

Any argument that takes one of these forms is a valid deductive argument. The name of the first form, *modus ponens* (often abbreviated MP), means "mode of affirming." It gets this name because it affirms a condition (*A*) that would guarantee the conclusion (*B*). Stated differently, it says that if *A* is true, then *B* is true; *A* is true; therefore *B* is also true. Notice that this fits perfectly with our established description of a valid deductive argument: even if one or more of the premises is false, the argument is still valid; if the premises are true, the conclusion is certainly true; and all the information in the conclusion is already contained in the premises. The example argument above about George W. Bush becoming the forty-third president of the United States took the form of MP. We could also rework our old argument about Socrates to fit this form:

If Socrates is a man, he is mortal.

Socrates is a man.

Therefore, Socrates is mortal.

The name of the second form, *modus tollens* (often abbreviated MT), means "mode of denying." It is given this name because it seeks to deny the content in the conclusion by denying a condition that is necessary to guarantee the conclusion. Stated differently, MT begins the same way as MP by saying that if *A* is true, then *B* is also true; but then it denies that *B* is true, which leads to the conclusion that *A* must not be true. Here is a common argument for God's existence that takes the form of MT:

If God does not exist, then objective moral values do not exist.

Objective moral values do exist.

Therefore, God exists.[4]

In this example, we see the form of MT. In the first premise, *A* is "God does not exist"; *B* is "Objective moral values do not exist." In the second premise, "not *B*" is "It is not true that objective moral values do not exist," and when we eliminate the double negative, it

---

4. This version of the moral argument appears in many places in the work of William Lane Craig.

becomes more simply "Objective moral values do exist." In the conclusion, "not *A*" is "It is not true that God does not exist," or more simply "God exists."

Inductive Arguments

We have shown that one key feature of a valid deductive argument is that if the premises are true, the conclusion must be true. We saw earlier in this chapter that the conclusion of a valid deductive argument cannot possibly be false (assuming all the premises are true). This leads us to one of the most important differences between deductive and inductive reasoning. In an inductive argument, even if the premises are all true, the conclusion is still not certain. While deductive arguments lead to a certain conclusion, inductive arguments lead only to a probable conclusion. Therefore, a valid inductive argument still has room for doubt as to whether the conclusion is true.

> Inductive arguments lead only to a probable conclusion. Therefore, a valid inductive argument still has room for doubt as to whether the conclusion is true.

One way to think of inductive reasoning is to think about the process of gathering good evidence to make a case. Even though you can't be 100 percent sure that the conclusion is true, a good inductive argument can give you many good reasons to think that the conclusion is indeed true.

To see the difference between this and a deductive argument, think back to a key feature of deductive arguments. We saw above that in a deductive argument the premises clearly state all the information we need in order to know that the conclusion is true. The conclusion of a deductive argument doesn't add any new information; instead, it restates the information already present in the premises. Our example argument about Socrates should refresh your memory about this point. The conclusion of the argument (Socrates is mortal) doesn't add any information. Instead, it is just the natural consequence of the information already presented in the premises. With those key points in mind, we can more easily see a difference in inductive arguments.

In inductive arguments a leap must be made. Good evidence is presented, but some information is still missing. Consider this example:

This horse has four legs.

That horse has four legs.

That other horse has four legs.

Therefore, all horses have four legs.

In this example, we see that even if all the premises are true, we still can't be 100 percent sure that the conclusion is true. A leap is made between the premises and the conclusion. We see that the three horses sampled do indeed give us good reason to think that "having four legs" is a common feature of all horses, not just these three. But even so, we can't be sure. The conclusion has information that is not contained in the premises: the conclusion of the example above makes a statement about all horses, even though we have actually seen only three horses. So we have been led to a probable conclusion, not a certain one.

Political polling results offer another example of an inductive argument. During a campaign for an election, you will often read something like, "Candidate x enjoys the support of 50 percent of all voters, while candidate y has the support of only 25 percent of the voters, and 25 percent are undecided." Let's say that the conclusion of the argument is that "50 percent of all voters support candidate x." The premises of the argument come from the raw polling data. Implied in the stated result is that the organization that polled the voters gathered results similar to the following:

Voter 1 expressed support for candidate x.

Voter 2 expressed support for candidate x.

Voter 3 expressed support for candidate y.

Voter 4 is undecided.

The polling organization presumably contacted more than just four voters, but however many they contacted, their results (in this example) show that half express support for candidate x. These data serve as the premises for the conclusion "50 percent of all voters support candidate *x*." As with all inductive arguments, however, we can't be sure that the conclusion is true. The polling company surveyed a relatively small number of voters and then assumed the population at large would express support for candidates in similar proportions to those actually surveyed. So the data is presented as evidence supporting the conclusion, but the conclusion is far from certain.

In looking at these two examples of inductive arguments (the horse argument and the polling data argument), we can see another feature of inductive arguments: they can be made stronger by adding more evidence. Think back again to deductive arguments for a moment. Remember that deductive arguments are all-or-nothing: all the information in the conclusion is already expressed in the premises, so if the premises are true, then we are 100 percent certain that the conclusion is true. In that sense, deductive arguments cannot have varying degrees of strength or weakness. But inductive arguments can, and one of the most obvious ways to improve the strength of an inductive argument is to increase the number of premises that provide evidence supporting the conclusion. In the example argument about horses having four legs, our argument becomes stronger if we count the legs on more horses. Likewise, we can be more confident in the accuracy of the political poll if the polling organization samples a larger number of voters. The polling argument can also be strengthened in other ways: sampling voters from diverse geographical regions, contacting voters at different times of the day (normal work hours during the week, and also evenings and weekends, for example), using different methods to contact voters (landlines and cell phones, for example), and so on. All of these methods would make a stronger case for a conclusion that intends to say something about "all voters."

Now that we have described the basic features of inductive argumentation, we should note one common misunderstanding about inductive arguments. Sometimes inductive reasoning is described as reasoning "from particulars to a universal." To reason inductively, it is said, we examine the similarity of particular items, and then from this similarity we are able to arrive at a universal principle. Here is an example:

Plato was a man, and he was mortal.
Socrates was a man, and he was mortal.

> Aristophanes was a man, and he was mortal.
>
> Every other man that I know about is mortal.
>
> Therefore, all men are mortal.

Notice, first, that this fits the description of inductive reasoning quite well: an accumulation of evidence points to a conclusion; the conclusion is only probable, not certain; and the conclusion contains information that is not explicit in the premises. Second, it does indeed seem to be reasoning from particulars to universals. If all individual men observed are mortal, then we could safely conclude that all men are mortal. The particular item is the mortality of the individual men, and the universal principle is the claim that all men are mortal. The same could be said of both the horse argument and the polling data argument above.

But inductive reasoning doesn't always go from particulars to universals. Here is an example:

> All dogs are mortal.
>
> All cats are mortal.
>
> All bears are mortal.
>
> Etc.
>
> Therefore, this creature is also probably mortal, even though I have no idea what kind of creature this is.

Here again, this example fits nicely with the description of inductive reasoning. It is based on the accumulation of evidence that leads to a probable (but not certain) conclusion, and the conclusion contains new information that is not stated in the premises. But this argument does not go from particulars to universals. In fact, it goes the other way: it begins with several universal principles and concludes with a particular individual fact. So while you may hear people say that inductive reasoning draws universal principles from particular observations, keep in mind that this is not always the case.

Laws of Logic

In a chapter dealing with the basics of reasoning, it is worth mentioning a little more about logic. For those who have not had formal training in the subject, logic can seem to be somewhat mysterious and perhaps esoteric. But in truth, logic is one of the most practical branches of philosophy. Logic is the study of good reasoning, and it is likely that you already grasp basics of logic just through your own common sense and innate reasoning abilities. As we think about good reasoning and good arguments, the most basic and fundamental principles of logic are often summed up in what are called the *three laws of logic* or sometimes the *three laws of thought*: iden-tity, *noncontradiction*, and *the excluded middle*. These three laws should probably be called *principles of common-sense reasoning* because they appeal to basic principles of reasoning that just about everyone is aware of. Most people might not think about, study, and analyze these principles quite like philosophers do, so a brief examination of them can help us see that they are part of the very fabric of what we call *common sense*.

> The three principles of common-sense reasoning are the law of identity, the law of noncontradiction, and the law of the excluded middle.

The Law of Identity

The *law of identity* says that whatever something is, that is what it is. Simple, right? The law of identity is so basic that almost everyone is able to grasp it on the first try. Logicians will sometimes describe the law of identity by using a letter of the alphabet like this: *A* is *A*. That means for any object (*A*), that object is what it is (*A*) and not something else. This is just a formal way of pointing out what should be fairly obvious: things are what they are.

We can describe it another way. In addition to saying that things are what they are, we can also say that things *exist in particular ways*. Think about the book you are reading right now (assuming you aren't reading a digital copy): the book has a particular size and shape, it has a particular number of pages with particular words on them, and the cover has a particular design. Maybe it has a mark on this page from your pencil or pen, and perhaps a page or two has been folded over at the corner. The point is that to understand what the book is (the one you are holding in your hands), you can observe all the particulars of what it is like. If the book wasn't exactly like that in every way, then it wouldn't be *that* book. It would be something else (perhaps a different book, or something else altogether). And this doesn't just apply to books; it also applies to everything else: horses, trees, my sister's cat, my love for my mother, or your hopes for the future. Each of these things exists in a particular way, and all of the particulars about the way something exists describe that thing's *identity*.

> The law of identity says that *A* is *A*.

Sometimes those who criticize the law of identity will do so by suggesting that it is nothing more than an empty exercise in repetition—as the song from the old TV show says, "A horse is a horse, of course, of course." But that isn't quite what the law of identity is doing. It isn't just repeating "a horse is a horse" or "a book is a book." Instead, the idea here is to point to the *particular ways* in which a *particular thing* exists. So when this principle is described by saying "*A* is *A*," the first *A* stands for the object or item in question (like "this particular book"), and the second *A* stands for the particular ways in which that particular book exists. This, after all, is how we know what something is. If it weren't for the law of identity, we wouldn't be able to pick out objects or ideas and differentiate them from other objects and ideas. If the law of identity didn't apply, and things didn't exist in particular ways, then a meaningful understanding of the world around us would be impossible.

The law of identity should be obvious to everyone. It is common sense; almost everyone grasps intuitively the principle that things are what they are. When we make arguments, however, we can occasionally make mistakes regarding identity. It is hard, after all, to make a good argument about what "the church fathers believed," for example, if we aren't sure who we are talking about or in what century they lived. Bad arguments may contain confusions of identity, but good arguments always clearly identify things as they are.[5]

---

5. In popular culture, *identity* sometimes refers only to what we call something, or how it is perceived to be, or some other subjective quality. Here, as with most discussions on logic, a thing's identity is what it actually is, not what we call it or what we perceive it to be.

The Law of Noncontradiction

Closely related to the law of identity (and just as important for meaningful understanding of the world) is the *law of noncontradiction*. (In some contexts this principle is called the law of contradiction, which could be confusing.) Like the law of identity, the law of noncontradiction also points to the particular ways things exist—their color, size, or shape, for example. These are called *properties*. Something that is blue, for example, has the property of *being blue*. The law of noncontradiction says that an object that has the property *being blue* cannot at the same time and in the same sense also have the property *not being blue*. Just as with the law of identity, logicians sometimes use letters of the alphabet to express the law of noncontradiction: For any object x and any property F, x cannot be both F and not-F at the same time and in the same sense. God cannot be both omnipotent and not omnipotent. A ball cannot be both blue and not blue.

A common attempt to deny the law of noncontradiction is to cite examples that seem to violate the principle but also seem to be true.

> The law of noncontradiction says that for any object x and any property F, x cannot be both F and not-F at the same time and in the same sense.

Consider, for example, a ball that is half blue and half white. Someone might say, "This ball is both blue and not blue at the same time." The solution here is just a matter of precision. To be more precise, it is not true that the ball is both blue and not blue. The truth is that half of the ball is blue and the other half of the ball is not blue. Someone else might cite Charles Dickens's famous opening line of the book *A Tale of Two Cities*: "It was the best of times, it was the worst of times." Recall that the law of noncontradiction asserts that any object cannot be both F and not-F *at the same time and in the same sense*. Dickens isn't contradicting himself because he means that it was the best of times in one sense and the worst of times in an entirely different sense. No matter what other kinds of examples like this are suggested, the solution is simple: be more precise in describing the properties, and you will see that the law of noncontradiction always applies.

Another way to think about the law of noncontradiction is that for any proposition *P*, *P* and not-*P* cannot both be true at the same time and in the same sense. Framed in this way, we see that *P* and not-*P* are contradictory propositions. The law of noncontradiction applied to this tells us that these two contradictories cannot both be true.

The law of noncontradiction can be a very helpful tool in evaluating arguments. A contradiction in an argument always tells us that the argument is bad. As soon as we spot a contradiction in an argument, we can be sure that either (a) the conclusion is false or (b) the reasons provided cannot possibly support the conclusion. Good arguments, however, do not contain contradictions, and they do not fall prey to the naive objections that are sometimes offered against the law of noncontradiction.

The Law of the Excluded Middle

Like the law of noncontradiction and the law of identity, the *law of the excluded middle* is a common-sense aspect of making good arguments. This principle follows from exactly the same common sense that helps us understand the law of noncontradiction. The law of noncontradiction asserts that *P* and not-*P* cannot both be true at the same time and in the same sense. The law of the excluded middle says that either *P* or not-*P* must be true. That is, for any proposition, either the proposition is true or its negation is true. This principle is called the excluded middle because it recognizes the common-sense idea that there is no middle ground between a proposition and its denial. There simply isn't anything between *P* and not-*P*. If we say, for example, that *P* is "God exists," the law of the excluded middle says that either "God exists" is true or its negation, "God does not exist," is true. There just are no other options between those two.

Implied by the law of the excluded middle (but not saying exactly the same thing) is the *principle of bivalence*. While the law of the excluded middle says that for any proposition *P*, either *P* or not-*P* is true, the principle of bivalence says that for any clear, unambiguous statement, that statement is either true or it is false. While this is not without controversy among logicians, it seems fairly obvious that a clear, unambiguous statement, such as "the earth is flat," must be either true or false. There is no middle ground between the two options. So if *P* is "the earth is flat," the law of the excluded middle says that either *P* or not-*P* must be true—either "the earth is flat" is true or "it is not the case that the earth is flat" is true. Bivalence, on the other hand, says that the statement "the earth is flat" is either true or false. The distinction here may seem subtle, and indeed some logicians deny that there is a difference. One reason for the controversy is that

> The law of the excluded middle says that either "God exists" is true or its negation, "God does not exist," is true.

some logicians think that for some stated propositions the law of the excluded middle applies but the principle of bivalence does not. We will leave it to you to further explore this controversy if you wish to better grasp the difference between the principle of bivalence and the law of the excluded middle. For our purposes, however, it will suffice to say that the principle expressed as the law of the excluded middle is (like the others) a matter of common sense.

Some may object to this principle on the grounds that many statements are ambiguous or have indeterminate meaning. Imagine this claim about our philosopher friend Socrates: "Socrates was bald." Those who object to the law of the excluded middle might point out that the top of Socrates's head was indeed bare, but he did have *some* hair on his head. So if *P* is "Socrates was bald," it seems we have a case with some middle ground: neither *P* nor not-*P* are true. It is not quite true that "Socrates was bald," nor is it true that "Socrates was not bald." This is a confusion of what it means to be bald, however, and not an example in which the principle of the excluded middle does not apply. If a precise definition is given about what it means to say that someone is "bald," the confusion disappears. If "bald" means "has no hair whatsoever on the scalp," then it is easy to see that either Socrates was bald or Socrates was not bald. Things are a certain way, or they are not. There is no middle ground between the two options. Good arguments therefore present clear statements that don't contain the kind of confusion that arises from ambiguity. Instead, good arguments contain statements that are either true or false.

Conclusion

In the section above we discussed the three laws of logic. By referring to these principles of reasoning as "laws," we are not suggesting that they are like rules enforced externally—like traffic laws are in place to make sure everyone drives safely and according to the same conventions. Instead, to say that the basic principles of logic are "laws" is more like when we talk about physical laws, such as the law of gravity or the law of conservation of mass. These physical laws are merely descriptions of the way the world works and are useful at predicting the way physical objects in the universe behave. This is also the case for the laws of logic—in the sense that they aren't merely conventions of behavior, they can't be abolished by a majority vote, and they don't depend on culture or religion. The laws of logic just tell us how good reasoning works, and they are universally applicable across all times and all cultures.

3

Fallacies

In chapter 1 we mentioned the common misunderstanding people have about what a fallacy is, and what it means to say that something is fallacious. In our culture, people commonly use the word *fallacy* when they really mean to say that something is false. If a person believes that the conclusion of an argument is false, that person will often say that the argument is fallacious. This represents an incorrect understanding of what a fallacy is and of what it means to say that an argument is fallacious. Contrary to the popular misunderstanding, a fallacy is simply a mistake or defect in reasoning, and a fallacious argument is one that makes a mistake or contains some kind of defect in its reasoning. When such a mistake is made, the premises of the argument (whether they are true or false) do not actually provide good reasons to think the conclusion is true (whether it really is true or not).

We hope it is clear to you by this point that if you want to make good arguments, you must avoid fallacies. If you are interested in persuading someone that your position is true, or that they should adopt a new belief or take a particular course of action, the arguments that you present can only be effective if you avoid mistakes in reasoning. If you are interested in supporting your conclusions through good arguments, then you must remember that reasons offered in a fallacious argument are no reasons at all. So you need to learn how to

31

avoid fallacies as you construct arguments—and if you inadvertently make such a mistake in reasoning, you need to know how to correct it. Additionally, if you want to evaluate arguments offered by others, you must be able to spot any fallacies so that you can think clearly about the ideas being presented and evaluate more carefully whether you should accept the conclusions of those arguments. Therefore, being able to identify and avoid fallacies is essential for critical thinking and for making good arguments. In this chapter we present several common fallacies so that you will learn how to spot them and how to avoid them.

Formal fallacies are those that make mistakes in how the argument is structured.

There are two kinds of fallacies: *formal* and *informal*. Formal fallacies are those that make mistakes in how the argument is structured. These are called *formal* because the defect is in the *form* of the argument. Informal fallacies, on the other hand, are not related to the form or structure of the argument but rather to the content or the meaning of words and phrases in the argument itself.

Formal Fallacies

In the last chapter, we introduced two common valid forms of deductive syllogisms: *modus ponens* (MP) and *modus tollens* (MT). Any argument that takes one of these forms is formally valid, no matter what the premises and conclusion are. Recall the modified example argument about Socrates we have been using throughout this book. It takes this form:

> If Socrates is a man, he is mortal.
> Socrates is a man.
> Therefore, Socrates is mortal.

Because this argument takes the form of MP, it is a formally valid argument. Also in the last chapter, we offered an example argument for God's existence based on the existence of objective moral values. This argument took the form of MT; therefore, it is formally valid.

There are many other valid forms of syllogistic arguments besides MP and MT, and if you take a course in logic, you will probably be exposed to many of them and learn the basics of how to recognize them. Just as there are many valid forms of syllogistic arguments, there are many formal fallacies. Here we want to mention just two. In both cases, these arguments will appear to be valid syllogisms at first glance, but through careful analysis we can see that they are formally invalid.

Affirming the Consequent

An *if . . . then* statement, like the ones that appear as the first premise in MP and MT, is called a *hypothetical proposition*. In other words, any statement that takes the form "if *A*, then *B*" is a hypothetical proposition. The first half of any such proposition is the *antecedent*, and the second half is the *consequent*. So for the statement "if *A*, then *B*," *A* is the antecedent and *B* is the consequent. In the example "If Socrates is a man, then he is mortal," the antecedent is "Socrates is a man," and the consequent is "he is mortal." In every such hypothetical proposition that takes the form "if *A*, then *B*," what is being said is that if *A* is true, then *B* is guaranteed to be true.

Recall that MP gets its name from a term that means "mode of affirming." It gets this name because it *affirms the antecedent* in order to show that the consequent must be true. We start with the hypothetical proposition (if *A*, then *B*), and then we affirm *A*; and since *A* guarantees *B*, then *B* must be true as well. That line of reasoning is perfectly valid. But sometimes in the course of using these kinds of hypotheticals to prove conclusions, we commit the fallacy called *affirming the consequent*. To the untrained eye, this fallacious form has the appearance of MP, but it isn't MP. Instead, it takes a different form that contains a serious defect in reasoning. The form of this fallacy is as follows:

If *A*, then *B*.
B.
Therefore, *A*.

This fallacy is so named because it affirms the consequent (*B*) of the hypothetical proposition in an attempt to prove the conclusion

(A). Here are a couple of example arguments that take this fallacious form:

> If Jesus is God, he can turn water into wine.
> Jesus can turn water into wine.
> Therefore, Jesus is God.

> If God inspired the Bible, then the Bible is true and trustworthy.
> The Bible is true and trustworthy.
> Therefore, God inspired the Bible.

Depending on your beliefs about Jesus, God, and the Bible, you might believe that the premises and conclusion of both arguments are true. Even if all of these statements are true (and we happen to think that they are), these two arguments contain a critical defect in reasoning: they commit the fallacy of affirming the consequent. In each case, they begin with a hypothetical proposition (if A, then B), but instead of affirming the antecedent (A) in order to prove the truth of the consequent (B), they attempt to prove the truth of the antecedent by affirming the consequent.

To see the problem more clearly, let's look at a simple example of this fallacy:

> If it is raining, the sidewalk is wet.
> The sidewalk is wet.
> Therefore, it is raining.

In this example we can immediately see what is wrong: the sidewalk could have become wet from any number of causes other than rain. Perhaps someone turned on the garden hose and aimed it at the sidewalk. Maybe a large chunk of ice was placed on the sidewalk and melted in the heat of the sun. The problem is this: just because rain guarantees that the sidewalk will be wet, it doesn't mean that the sidewalk being wet guarantees that it is raining. Said the other way around, you can't properly conclude that it is raining just because the sidewalk is wet—and the reason for this is that the sidewalk could have become wet from many other causes right in the middle of a bright, sunshine-filled, rain-free day!

Remember, though, that the fallacy has nothing to do with whether the statements are true. Instead, the fallacy is in the form. It *could* indeed be raining, and that *could* be the reason that the sidewalk is wet. The form is fallacious, however, because affirming the consequent cannot possibly *guarantee* the truth of the antecedent, as it purports to do. It would be a deductive argument with true premises and a false conclusion—something you can never have because true premises of a deductive argument guarantee the truth of the conclusion. Again, you can prove that the sidewalk is wet by affirming the fact that it is raining, but you can't prove that it is raining by affirming that the sidewalk is wet.

Now that we have analyzed this simple example, glance back up to the argument about Jesus turning water into wine. You'll notice that the argument attempts to prove the antecedent by affirming the consequent. But just as in the rain/sidewalk example, any number of other facts about Jesus could explain his ability to turn water into wine. He could have been a sorcerer, specializing in the conversion of water to other types of beverages. He could have been a mere mortal endowed by God with special powers to turn water into wine. Or he could in fact be God. The trouble is that you cannot prove that Jesus is God simply by affirming the consequent of the hypothetical—that he can turn water into wine. The same is true for the example about God inspiring the Bible. Just because something is true and trust-worthy does not mean it is God inspired. Of course, in any of these examples you could properly prove the consequent by affirming the antecedent. But to attempt to prove the antecedent by affirming the consequent is formally fallacious.

Denying the Antecedent

Recall that MT presents a hypothetical statement (if *A*, then *B*) and then denies the consequent (*B*) in order to prove that the antecedent (*A*) is not true. Let's say that a different way: The hypothetical means that if *A* is true, then *B* is guaranteed to be true. MT denies *B*. But since *A* guarantees *B*, denying *B* proves that *A* must be denied as well.

Just as with MP, an attempt to construct an argument of the form MT can go wrong, and a defect in reasoning can be introduced. The fallacy of *denying the antecedent* takes the following form, similar to MT, but formally invalid:

If *A*, then *B*.
Not *A*.
Therefore, not *B*.

This fallacy makes the mistake of denying the antecedent in an attempt to prove that the consequent must be denied. Here is an example argument that takes this fallacious form:

If God does not exist (*A*), then Christianity is false (*B*).
God does exist (not *A*).
Therefore, Christianity is true (not *B*).

When we attempt to put this into "if *A*, then *B*," we see that *A* is "God does not exist," and *B* is "Christianity is false." So "not *A*" means "God does exist," and "not *B*" means "Christianity is true (i.e., not false)." Here again, you may believe (as we do) that the premises and the conclusion of this argument are true. But the argument is clearly fallacious for this reason: while a denial of the consequent requires a denial of the antecedent (because the antecedent guarantees the consequent), a denial of the antecedent does *not* require a denial of the consequent.

We know this can seem complicated the first time you read it, so let's go back to thinking of rainy weather and wet sidewalks to see more clearly what is wrong here:

If it is raining, then the sidewalk is wet.
It is not raining.
Therefore, the sidewalk is not wet.

Do you see what is wrong? The sidewalk could indeed be wet, even if it is not raining. (Remember the garden hose and the chunk of ice?) Likewise with the earlier example: it could be the case that Christianity *is* false, even if God does exist. God's existence alone does not guarantee that Christianity is true.

Before we move on to informal fallacies, it is worth acknowledging that all the above material may have seemed confusing to you, especially if this is the first time you have read about these things. If so, you might need to review the above material several more times to make sure you understand the defect in reasoning in each of the two fallacies mentioned. It is quite possible that a person who has never heard of these fallacies can still spot the mistakes in reasoning, all the while not having any idea what they are called. In presenting this material, our primary goal is not to equip you to name the fallacies ("Aha! I have spotted an example of the fallacy of affirming the consequent!"). Rather, our goal is to help equip you to spot the actual mistake in reasoning ("Wait a minute! There are many possible causes for the sidewalk being wet. Just because it is wet doesn't mean it must be raining!"). Of course we can't fully equip you to do that for every possible mistake in reasoning, especially in such a short book as this. But we hope that the discussion of formal fallacies helps contribute to the process. The same is true as we discuss informal fallacies below. Being able to name the fallacies is good, but being able to identify the root of the mistake in reasoning and being able to avoid such mistakes in your own arguments are much more important.

Informal Fallacies

While formal fallacies make their mistakes in the form of the argument, informal fallacies make their mistakes in the content and the meaning of the content. A careful eye will see examples of formal fallacies in a wide variety of contexts, but many, if not most, of the fallacies we find will be informal. The reason for this, perhaps, is that informal fallacies are often very tempting to commit. They tend to lure us in, tempting us with an all-too-easy way to prove a conclusion that we so desperately want to prove. In the end, however, they are fatally defective and unable to help us accomplish our goals. For this reason we must learn to see them for what they are and to avoid them in our own arguments. While countless informal fallacies can be committed, we will mention just a few of the more common ones that you are likely to encounter (in your own thinking or in the arguments of others).

Begging the Question

The fallacy of *begging the question*,[1] also referred to by the Latin term *petitio principii*, is an example of circular reasoning. Reasoning in a circle means that you create an argument in which the truth of one or more premises depends on the truth of the conclusion. In other words, this fallacy makes the mistake of assuming in a premise what the argument itself is supposed to be proving. The following dialogue is commonly given as an example of this kind of mistake in reasoning:

Sam: God exists.

Joe: Why should I believe that?

Sam: Because the Bible tells us that he does.

Joe: Why should I believe the Bible tells the truth?

Sam: Because the Bible is God's Word, and God cannot lie.

This is fallacious, and an example of circular reasoning, because the truth of the last two premises "the Bible is God's Word" and "God cannot lie" both depend on the conclusion being true ("God exists"). Here is another example: "I know that God exists because of the many wonderful blessings he has given me." This is circular because God can only give blessings if he exists. One more example:

It is impossible that God exists. We know this conclusively because the entire universe is composed of physical matter. While it is possible that somewhere in the unexplored physical universe there may be a very great and powerful being, those who believe in God claim that he is an immaterial, spiritual being. But because only physical, material things exist, we can conclude that it is not just unlikely that God exists—it is impossible.

This is the kind of thing that a scientific naturalist might say.[2] While this example is a bit more subtle than the others, it is still circular: to prove the conclusion that God (an immaterial, spiritual being)

1. In everyday conversation, people often use the phrase "begs the question" to mean something entirely different. Usually they mean something like, "If such and such is true, that just leads us to the obvious question . . ."

2. Scientific naturalism is the view that only physical, material things exist and that the methods of science are the only methods that can lead us to knowledge

cannot exist, the one proposing this argument first assumes that only physical, material things exist.

Unfortunately, circular reasoning is quite common because it is very tempting (as we suggest above). If we stop and consider the psychology behind this kind of argument, we can probably (sympathetically) see what is going on. Long before Sam attempts to construct an argument to prove to Joe that God exists, Sam already believes that God exists. The belief in the truth of the conclusion comes before the argument is ever offered. Since Sam already believes that God exists, the argument he constructs *seems* to be quite reasonable. Without giving it much thought, Sam takes it for granted that God exists because he is already convinced that God exists—so it doesn't seem inappropriate at all to construct premises in an argument that take for granted that God exists. The same is true for our scientific naturalist friend: before he attempts to construct the argument, he already believes that non-physical beings cannot possibly exist. So of course it doesn't *seem to him* that he is making a mistake in reasoning when he offers an argument that depends on the conclusion being true.

> While formal fallacies make their mistakes in the form of the argument, informal fallacies make their mistakes in the content and the meaning of the content.

Avoiding this fallacy in our own arguments is a simple matter of critical self-reflection. If we learn to honestly assess what we believe as we develop arguments to support these beliefs, we will be less likely to inadvertently engage in circular reasoning. Any time we do argue in a circle, we are not really giving any good reasons to support the conclusion.

Ad Hominem

The *ad hominem* fallacy is committed when an argument is directed at a person, instead of at a line of reasoning, in an effort to

---

about the universe. A scientific naturalist is a person who believes that scientific naturalism is true.

show that the opponent's conclusion or conclusions are incorrect. The name of this fallacy comes to us from Latin and means "to the man." This fallacy is a kind of personal attack; but since personal attacks are (unfortunately) common in our culture, we must note that not all personal attacks are fallacious. Here is an example of the *ad hominem* fallacy:

> Raising the minimum wage is good for our economy. Of course the powerful CEO of the major corporation would *say* that raising the minimum wage is bad for the economy because he is motivated by nothing more than greed and pure profit!

The reason this is fallacious is that the motivations of the CEO are irrelevant to determining the question of whether raising the minimum wage is good for the economy. The person making this argument is simply attacking the motives of the CEO, without providing any relevant reasons to help us determine whether the conclusion is true or false. Even if the CEO *is* motivated by greed and profit, that fact has nothing to do with whether raising the minimum wage is good for the economy. The CEO may be able to present good arguments supporting the claim that raising the minimum wage would harm the economy. So to avoid the *ad hominem* fallacy, his opponent would need to go after the premises and reasoning within that argument rather than attacking the motives of the CEO.

It can be tempting to commit this fallacy, especially if we really do think that our opponent is of questionable character or has impure motives, and especially if we really do think that the claim the person is offering is false. If we want to make good arguments, however, we must examine our own line of reasoning carefully to make sure that we are not appealing to irrelevant motivations on the part of our opponent in our attempt to prove that our opponent's claim is false.

As we have already suggested, not all personal attacks are fallacious. There are at least two circumstances in which it would not be fallacious to attack the character or motives of a person: when the character or motives of the person are relevant, or when the attack is not offered as a reason to reject a claim. First, a situation could arise in which a person's character or motives are relevant to the question under consideration. An example of this would be a court case in which a witness was called to give a testimony. It is not fallacious for opposing counsel to attack the character or motives of the witness in those cases in which the court is relying on the character and motives of the witness as evidence that the testimony is true. Second, it would also not be fallacious to simply make a personal attack against someone without using that attack to suggest that a conclusion is false. If you are in a public debate against an opponent, it would not be fallacious for you to begin your opening statement by attacking the character and motives of your opponent as long as you are not offering your attack as a reason that your audience should reject your opponent's conclusion. Perhaps such a move would be impolite, but it would not be an example of fallacious reasoning.

Ad Populum

Like the *ad hominem* fallacy, the *ad populum* fallacy is fallacious because it asserts something that is irrelevant to the argument. It gets its name from Latin, meaning "to the people," and is an appeal to the popularity of a claim in an attempt to show that the claim is true: since so many people believe the claim, the claim must be true. This fallacy is often committed in the context of religious claims: "So many people, in so many places and across the ages, have believed in God. God must exist!" This is clearly fallacious, because the number of people who believe the claim that God exists is irrelevant to the truth of the claim. Here are a few other examples:

- Because so many people oppose a tax increase, that policy must be bad for the country.
- The president was elected by an overwhelming majority; there- fore, he must be the right man for the job.
- Nine out of ten dentists recommend this brand of chewing gum, so chewing it must not have any negative effects on dental health.
- Almost all Christians throughout the last two thousand years have believed that Jesus is God, so it must be true.

In each of these examples, you can see that the appeal made "to the people" is not relevant to whether the claim is true or false. Be- cause these appeals are not relevant to the claim, they are examples of fallacious reasoning. It must be noted, however, that not all appeals to popularity are fallacious. For example, if the claim is "Candidate A will win the election," then appealing to the fact that a majority of respondents in the poll said that they were going to vote for candidate A *is* relevant; so appealing to the people in this sense is not fallacious. Making these kinds of appeals is also appropriate in sociological studies. Sociologists often focus on describing what is true of groups of people or cultures, and in the process of doing that, it is perfectly appropriate to appeal to what is true about "most people" in that group or culture. It is always fallacious, however, when we appeal to the popularity of a belief or claim in our efforts to show that the claim is true.

Inappropriate Appeal to Authority

Sometimes appeals are made to an authority figure: because an expert thinks that the claim is true, the claim must be true. In some cases this can be perfectly appropriate; relying on expert opinion can be a reliable way to determine whether certain claims are true or false. In many cases, however, the fact that the person is an authority figure is irrelevant to the claim under consideration. In such cases the appeal to authority is inappropriate and fallacious. One of the most common contexts for this fallacy to occur is in advertisements: a famous person tells us that a product is good, and that person's testimony is presented as a reason to think that the product is good. This is fallacious when the person's fame is irrelevant to the question of whether the product is any good, such as when a famous athlete promotes a specific brand of razors, clothing, or pizza. This fallacy also arises when Hollywood stars are called to testify before Congress about an issue outside their area of expertise. These kinds of appeals are fallacious because they assert (sometimes implicitly, sometimes explicitly) that the person's fame is a good reason to accept their claim as being true.

Though it is fallacious to appeal to an authority figure for matters that lie outside that person's area of expertise, in some cases it can be quite tempting to do this. In debates about God's existence, for example, a theistic scholar is often paired with an atheistic scientist.

In the aftermath of these debates, the audience can be tempted to appeal to the authority or expertise of one or the other debate participants. While the scientist, for example, may be an expert in her particular field of science, that expertise does not extend to other fields, such as philosophy or theology. Likewise, the theist may be a well-recognized expert in the philosophy of religion, but his expertise may not extend to scientific matters. Richard Dawkins (an atheist who is a recognized expert in zoology and evolutionary biology) is no more qualified to evaluate the philosophical arguments for God's existence than any other nonexpert. Likewise, William Lane Craig (a theist who is a recognized expert in philosophy) is no more qualified to evaluate some established principle in the field of genetics than any other nonexpert. While each of these men enjoys expertise in his field, it would be fallacious for someone to appeal to that authority to defend the truth of a claim that lies outside that field of expertise.

Genetic Fallacy

The *genetic fallacy*, sometimes called the fallacy of origins,[3] is an attempt to prove false (or true) an idea based on the source of that idea. We commonly see this fallacy arise in debates about God's existence or about the truth of some particular religious viewpoint. Atheists, for example, will often point out that people raised in predominantly Christian cultures will come to believe that Christianity is true, while people raised in Muslim countries will come to believe that Islam is true. The claim is then made that Christianity (or Islam) must be false because it can be shown that people believe in a particular religion only because that is what they were taught to believe. This line of reasoning is clearly fallacious, however. How a person came to believe that Christianity is true is irrelevant to the question of whether Christianity is actually true. Of course this kind of fallacious reasoning can go both ways: Christianity is true because that is what my parents taught me. Here again, the origin of the belief doesn't help us determine whether the belief is actually true.

3. The "genesis" of something is its origin.

False Dilemma

Sometimes referred to as black-and-white thinking, the *false dilemma* is a fallacious line of reasoning that inappropriately suggests that a question has only two possible answers and that a choice must be made between those two, when in actuality more than two possible answers are available. For example, someone might say, "If you don't support prayer in public school, you must be an atheist." This is fallacious because it falsely suggests that there are only two options for any of us: either I support prayer in public school or I'm an atheist. But clearly these are not the only two choices: a theist may oppose prayer in public school, and (perhaps) an atheist could support it.

This fallacy also occurs in some areas of controversy in which two positions in the controversy are habitually emphasized to the exclusion of other options. For example, in Christian theology it might be said, "You are either a Calvinist or an Arminian." In politics, people sometimes act as if you are either a Republican or a Democrat.[4] In each of these examples, a highly controversial issue (or set of issues) has resulted in the polarization of opponents into one of two major camps that tend to dominate the debate. To present these as if they were the only options available is fallacious.

It is important to note that not all dilemmas are false, so presenting a dilemma is not always fallacious. It is a true dilemma to say, "You are either a Calvinist or not a Calvinist," for example, or, "You are either a Republican or not a Republican." In these examples, the principle of bivalence is brought to bear: for any statement, it is either true or false. In other cases, only two options are available: "If you are going to make a turn, you must turn either to the right or to the left." So we see that a dilemma is only false, and therefore an element in faulty reasoning, if more than two options are available.

---

4. In contemporary American politics, this issue is often presented as a false trilemma: Democratic, Republican, or Independent. Unfortunately, this does nothing more than compound the faulty reasoning and further contribute to political confusion. The trilemma falsely assumes that people who belong to either the Democratic or the Republican parties are not independent—they don't have their own ideas, don't act out of their own self-interest, or only vote according to what party leaders dictate. It also fails to take into consideration sophisticated, well-reasoned, and well-developed political theories and positions that do not correspond well to the platforms of either of the two major parties.

Straw Man

Muhammad Ali is widely recognized as the greatest boxer of his time and one of the greatest heavyweight boxers who ever entered the ring. Which would be an easier task for you to achieve: surviving a twelve-round bout against Muhammad Ali . . . or surviving a twelve-round bout against a life-sized inflatable doll that looks like Muhammad Ali? The difference between those feats helps us to understand what the straw man fallacy is. The *straw man fallacy* is one in which you create an intentionally weakened, distorted, or obviously false version of your opponent's argument, and then attack that version specifically because it is easier for you to defeat than the real thing. You know you can't defeat Muhammad Ali, so you put up the life-sized inflatable in Muhammad Ali's place and then punch away. This fallacy is so named because, similar to an inflatable doll, it has in mind Muhammad Ali's clothes stuffed with straw rather than Muhammad Ali himself. This strategy is fallacious because it misrepresents your opponent's argument in an effort to prove that your opponent's claim is false. To correct this fallacy, you need to address your opponent's actual argument, because that is what your opponent is using to support the claim.

Red Herring

The *red herring fallacy* is an intentional distraction away from relevant issues. The name comes from a kind of fish (usually a herring, we suppose) that was strongly cured or smoked so that it emits an unpleasant, powerful aroma (that is, it stinks). If you are thinking or talking about something important, it is easy to be distracted if someone starts waving a smelly fish around. This fallacy occurs any time a person introduces a new concept that is not immediately relevant to the argument or claim under consideration for the purpose of distracting the audience or shifting the discussion away from an undesired result. For example, if the question under consideration is whether abortion is immoral, it would be a red herring to say, "I don't think abortion is immoral; and anyway, we have a problem with overpopulation as it is. What we really should be concerned about is proper distribution of resources to eliminate poverty." Here, a new idea is introduced (distribution of resources to eliminate poverty) specifically as a distraction designed to divert attention from the actual question (whether abortion is immoral). While it may be tempting to insert such distractions into a debate, it is always fallacious to do so.

Conclusion

Each of the fallacies above has a common element that makes the reasoning fallacious: they present reasons we should accept a claim as true, but these reasons turn out not to be good reasons at all. In most cases the reasons don't give us anything by which we can begin to determine whether the claim is true or false. This is what it means for an argument to be fallacious: the premises (reasons given) do not have the proper connection to the conclusion (the claim). As you strive to learn how to craft good arguments, it is necessary to make note of the more common and tempting ways in which our reasoning can go wrong. To make good arguments, you must avoid fallacies. While we have described some of the most common fallacies in this chapter, we could have named many more, and we encourage you to continue your study of common fallacies in arguments. The more fallacies you are aware of, the more likely it is you will avoid them in your thinking and in your arguments.

4

Belief, Fact, and Opinion

"You are entitled to your own opinion, but not to your own facts!" This is a well-known quip commonly heard in heated debates about politics or other emotionally charged issues. While the phrase is perhaps overused, it does indeed point to an important distinction that must be made in the context of argumentation: the difference between fact and opinion.

At first glance, this seems to be a simple and straightforward distinction that everyone understands. We all know the difference between fact and opinion, right? Surprisingly, a quick internet search reveals diversity of opinions about what these two words mean and how they relate to argument and debate, with many of the viewpoints expressed being entirely incompatible with one another. One perspective on "opinion," for example, is that it is purely a matter of personal preference, like a favorite color or preferred flavor of ice cream. Others think that an opinion is a judgment of reason based on fact, like assessing evidence in order to determine what best explains the sidewalk being wet. Some say that a fact is something that is objectively true. Others say that a fact is something that can be either true or false and that an opinion can be neither true nor false. Sometimes an opinion is said to be something a person "believes is true," whereas a fact is something that we can "know." Others distinguish fact and opinion on the basis of the subject matter: morals and religion (questions such as whether God exists, whether Jesus rose from the dead, or whether abortion is immoral) deal exclusively with matters of opinion, whereas science (issues such as the age of the earth, the mechanisms of evolution, or the molecular weight of hydrogen) deals exclusively with matters of fact. What at first seemed to be a simple distinction now appears quite confusing.

It is our belief that this distinction shouldn't be confusing, and we want to do what we can to make it less so. Our goal in this chapter is to reframe the fact/opinion distinction in terms of claims that are either *subjective* or *objective*. When we look at it this way, we can see that good arguments focus primarily on objective claims and are crafted in such a way that the audience understands the objectivity of the matters under discussion in the argument. As we engage with these ideas, we hope that you come away with a better understanding of the fact/opinion distinction; but more important, we want you to have a good grasp of how to properly leverage the subjective/objective distinction in order to make good arguments.

Subjective versus Objective

In the most basic sense, *objective claims* are those that can be proven true or false because they pertain to matters of the external world. Subjective claims, on the other hand, are claims about matters of personal preference. You can also think of objective claims as those dealing with matters that are public (things that other people can observe), while subjective claims deal with matters that are private (nonobservable things like emotions, sensations, or states of mind). For example, the claim that "there is a pineapple on the table" is objective, because it points to publicly accessible features of the world that other people can examine and investigate in order to determine if the claim is true or false. Even if we can't immediately observe the relevant data (say, the pineapple is on a table a hundred miles away), we could at the very least come up with a method to determine if the claim is true or false (such as traveling to the location to look). If someone makes the claim that "pineapple tastes sweet," on the other hand, that person is making a subjective claim. It is subjective because it pertains to a private sensation that is experienced only by the person who is making the claim, and because there is no way for anyone to examine anything to determine whether the claim is true or false. In the case of this claim, we couldn't even come up with a theoretical method for testing whether the claim is true

Objective claims are those that can be proven true or false because they pertain to matters of the external world. Subjective claims, on the other hand, are claims about matters of personal preference.

or false. Of course these descriptions are a bit oversimplified, but they are sufficient to get us going in the right direction to understand why this is important when we talk about claims made in arguments.

Beliefs, Claims, and Knowledge

Admittedly, the word *belief* has a fairly wide range of possible meanings and connotations. In chapter 1 we mentioned briefly that we tend to use the words *claims* and *beliefs* interchangeably. The reason for this, we said, is that when we express our beliefs verbally, they come out in the form of claims. For example, if you believe that the capital of Pennsylvania is Harrisburg, and you want to communicate this belief to another person, you will probably say something like, "The capital of Pennsylvania is Harrisburg." Since claims are a key feature of arguments, we are leaning heavily on one particular idea of what we mean when we say "belief." In this context, a belief is something that can be expressed as a claim and that reflects some feature of the world that the speaker takes to be true. In other words, a belief that you have is like a mental picture of the way you think the world is (for example, that the city of Harrisburg really is the capital city of Pennsylvania). The claim, on the other hand, is when you actually state that belief to someone else, either verbally or in writing. The belief is the way you think the world is, and the claim is nothing more than the belief expressed in words.

This is simple enough, but an interesting feature of human psychology has wreaked havoc on this simple concept. For some reason or another, people have begun to use the word *believe* in an entirely different way than what we just described, and with a significantly different connotation. The newfangled sense of the word can be seen in expressions like this: "Beliefs are matters of personal, subjective opinions, while knowledge is a matter of public, objective fact." Do you see what is happening here? To help us better understand what is happening, we turn to a brief lesson in *epistemology*, the study of knowledge.

A Brief Lesson in Epistemology

Traditionally understood, *knowledge* is when a person holds a belief for good reasons and that belief is true. This understanding is often described in terms of "justified true belief." Three elements are said to be essential for knowledge. First, knowledge begins with belief. Whatever else you think about beliefs, it seems fairly obvious that you cannot possibly *know* that Harrisburg is the capital of Pennsylvania unless you also *believe* that Harrisburg is the capital of Pennsylvania. Second, belief alone is not enough for knowledge; you also need to have *good reasons* that support the belief. If you believe that Harrisburg is the capital of Pennsylvania, but you came to that belief by randomly selecting it from a list of cities, then you just made a lucky guess. You didn't really know. To know it, you have to have good reasons that support your belief. Finally, to count as knowledge, your belief needs to be true. You can't possibly know that Pittsburgh is the capital of Pennsylvania . . . because it isn't. You can only know something if it is true. You can't possibly know something if it is false (even if you believe it). While some philosophers have suggested that you need more than these three

> Traditionally understood, "knowledge" is when a person holds a belief for good reasons and that belief is true. This understanding is often described in terms of "justified true belief."

elements to have knowledge, at the very least these are the minimum requirements. So, for our purposes, knowledge is *belief* that is held for *good reasons* and is *true*.

Let's put a magnifying glass over a couple of those elements in knowledge theory. Notice that in our description in the above paragraph, we described truth by using an example: the claim "Harrisburg is the capital of Pennsylvania" is true. But why is this claim true? In this case, it is true because Harrisburg really is the capital of Pennsylvania. Moreover, this is an *objective claim*. If someone heard you make that claim, they could easily work out a method by which they could determine whether the claim is true or false (they could speak with the governor of Pennsylvania, consult official public records, etc.). Everything they would need in order to determine whether it is true or false is publicly accessible. Moreover, if the claim is true, then it is objectively true.

Let's take a closer look at the role reasons play in all of this. Reasons, as we have seen, are what make us think our belief is true. Most of the time, the question isn't quite as simple as which city is the capital of Pennsylvania. Because many beliefs can be about complex matters, the reasons we have for those beliefs can have varying degrees of strength; some reasons can be better than others. On top of that, if we are relying on inductive reasoning,[1] no matter how many good reasons we come up with, at some point we have to make a leap. We can't be 100 percent sure whether the belief is true or false. Depending on the belief in question and the reasons offered, we can have varying degrees of certainty about whether the belief is true or false.

With that brief discussion of knowledge, we can now return to discussing how the word *belief* is commonly used.

Beliefs: A Common Understanding of the Concept

Because we cannot be 100 percent certain whether many of our beliefs are true, it can be tempting to overemphasize their subjective, private nature. When the subjective nature of beliefs is overemphasized,

1. See chap. 2. Recall that inductive reasoning relies on the accumulation of evidence that leads to a probable conclusion. The nature of inductive reasoning includes the idea that our conclusions are always less than 100 percent certain.

people will sometimes (mistakenly) refer to beliefs as *only* matters of subjective opinion. Elementary school students are often taught to differentiate fact from opinion, and sometimes they are told that the word *believe* is an indication that a person is stating her or his opinion. But this is clearly incorrect. While the belief itself is something subjective and private, the matter about which the belief is concerned can be either subjective or objective. In other words, beliefs can be either matters of fact or matters of opinion. You can believe that Harrisburg is the capital of Pennsylvania, and can you believe that chocolate ice cream is the best. Both of those beliefs are held privately and subjectively in your own mind. But clearly your belief about Harrisburg is a matter of objective fact while your belief about chocolate ice cream is about your personal, private taste and preference. Beliefs represent the way you think the world is; they can be matters of objective fact or subjective opinion, and when you state them, you make a claim. Corresponding to whether your beliefs are subjective or objective, your claims about those beliefs can be either subjective or objective. So it seems that the newfangled way of using the word *belief* is entirely mistaken.

Is Truth Subjective or Objective?

This new personal, subjective connotation of the word *belief* in contemporary culture has arisen alongside confusion about another concept: truth. In fact, it might be that as you read our brief epistemology lesson above, *you* objected to the way we were talking about claims being true or false. Indeed, we are confident that *many* people in our culture would object to our description of epistemology—not because our analysis is faulty but because (they would say) our concept of truth is faulty. They would say that truth is always relative to the person making the claim (a view sometimes called "truth relativism," which generally refers to the view that truth is subjective).[2] In this understanding of truth, claims can be *true for you* without being *true for others*. If you make a claim such as "Harrisburg is the capital of

2. When people talk about *relativism* with regard to truth, a more precise term to use would be *subjectivism*, because the idea is that truth is relative to the individual person.

Pennsylvania," for example, that claim might be true *for you* but not for someone else. This view of truth is connected to the idea that belief is always something private, an internal mental state. Belief is (in that sense) subjective. The trouble arises, however, if we start there and then conclude that because a belief itself is subjective, the claim is also subjective, and the truth of the matter is also subjective. If you take seriously anything we have said so far about arguments, this view of truth should seem quite strange.

This view of truth can lead to some awkward consequences. We will name just three. First, if truth is subjective (or relative), then science is impossible. The entire scientific enterprise depends on both reality and truth being objective; it requires that we can observe reality outside of ourselves, that we can test it and develop theories about how it works. All of this would be impossible if we could never say that anything we discover through scientific means is true (in the objective sense). Second, if truth is subjective, there is no such thing as morality. The concepts of right and wrong are reduced to matters of private, subjective preference, and we can never say that anything (murder, genocide, greed, slavery) is really wrong (for all people). Finally (and most relevant to this book), if truth is subjective, arguments are both impossible and unnecessary.

Objective Claims and Good Arguments

You may have noticed that instead of providing you with an argument for why the subjective view of truth must be wrong, the best we could do in the previous paragraph was to highlight some of the negative consequences. This is because if truth is subjective, then *our claim* about the nature of truth is also subjective; and, as we can now see, arguments are no good in defending subjective claims. No matter what reasons we can name, the person who holds to a subjective view of truth can always respond with, "Well, that may be true *for you*, but it isn't true *for me*." But arguments are also inadequate for any subjective claim, even if we think that truth is objective. Can you imagine trying to defend your claim that "chocolate ice cream is the most delicious"? Claims like these really are subjective: they pertain only to matters of personal, private preference, and are not about anything objective in the world. Because these claims are subjective, no arguments are available to defend them. Imagine trying to persuade me to adopt the belief that "chocolate ice cream is the most delicious." What supporting reasons could you provide? Would you give an inductive argument or a deductive argument? The answer is that any attempt to craft an argument to defend this (or any other) subjective claim will always be fruitless.

The reason arguments about subjective claims are fruitless should be easy to see, and if truth itself is subjective, then we should be able to see why arguments will always be pointless. If truth is subjective, then everything is opinion; every opinion is "true" for the one who holds it, so all beliefs are equally "true." If all beliefs are equally true, then there is no need to try to persuade someone to change their belief about anything—because the belief they have is already "true" for them. Some people think that only claims about certain topics are "relative," like religion or ethics, and we suspect that this is why some people say these topics are "matters of opinion." Saying that these topics are matters of opinion can be a covert way to avoid having to face well-reasoned arguments that may be presented about important issues in those fields.

Fact and Opinion

Taking everything we have said so far into consideration, let's return to the idea of defining fact and opinion. We think that a "fact" is something objective. Of course there are "facts" about your opinions. For example, it is an objective fact that you do have a subjective preference of what flavor of ice cream is most delicious. Such facts are objective because they are publicly available, and we have a method we can use to test whether the fact about the subjective preference is true or false. For example, we can ask you, "What flavor of ice cream do you think is most delicious?" Your answer will be definitive because you are a proper authority on your own personal preferences. We will then know that it is objectively true that you prefer one particular flavor. Despite this, we still think it makes more sense to reserve the word *fact* to refer only to facts about objective claims. If we want to develop and present good arguments, it won't do us much good if we dwell on facts about private, subjective preferences.

We think that "opinion," on the other hand, pertains only to the subjective. As we have acknowledged above, all beliefs are, in one way of looking at it, subjective. And in that sense, all beliefs are opinions. However, as we demonstrated, beliefs can be about either subjective things or objective things. You can have beliefs about your personal preference for an ice cream flavor, but you can (and do) have beliefs about a great many objective features of the world (like what city is the capital of Pennsylvania, for example). Given this distinction, then, we think it makes more sense to reserve the word *opinion* only for those cases in which we have a belief about something subjective (like what flavor of ice cream is most delicious). When we have a belief about something objective and want to craft and present a good argument, using the word *opinion* doesn't really help us accomplish this.

Good Arguments Make Objective, Factual Claims

With these new tools in our toolbox, we can conclude this chapter with a different kind of description of an argument and what function it serves. We can say that *an argument presents objective, factual claims for the purpose of persuading others to acknowledge certain facts about the world.* Two aspects of this description should be highlighted. First, arguments present objective, factual claims; arguments about matters of subjective opinion are pointless. As we said above, can you imagine trying to convince someone else that chocolate ice cream is the most delicious? Because things like this are purely subjective, it is impossible to provide an argument that could persuade someone else to adopt them. So, good arguments will not focus on matters of subjective opinion but instead will focus on objective matters of fact.

> An argument presents objective, factual claims for the purpose of persuading others to acknowledge certain facts about the world.

Second, we argue to persuade someone to acknowledge certain objective facts about the world. In a sense, we want our audience to see that one or more of their current beliefs do not match what is objectively true about the world. Sometimes when my beliefs and your beliefs conflict with one another, we are tempted to say, "You have your opinion; I have mine." But if our beliefs are about matters of objective fact (and if we have a desire to conform our beliefs to the way the world really is), then an argument is exactly what is necessary when my beliefs conflict with yours. If I want to know what the world is like, then I must be open to hearing arguments from others, even if those arguments cause me to face the uncomfortable possibility that my current beliefs don't align with the way the world really is. Likewise, if we want our audience to see that their beliefs don't align with the way the world really is, then we will want to create and present a good argument.

Conclusion

We hope that framing the discussion of "fact versus opinion" in terms of "objective versus subjective" has helped you see the distinctions that are important for making good arguments. Whenever there is a disagreement, it can be tempting to attribute this disagreement to differences of opinion. We hope you see, however, that this can create confusion, and we hope that the tools this chapter provided will help you cut through this confusion when you encounter it. Making good arguments depends, to a large degree, on being able to clearly articulate your claims as matters of objective fact.

5

Defining Your Terms

Have you ever been in a debate with someone who tries to "win" by simply looking up a word in a dictionary and pointing to the definition as the only proof needed to substantiate their point? This all-too-common tactic can be frustrating for everyone involved, especially when you are trying to have a meaningful discussion about your ideas (and not about dictionary definitions). If this ever happens to you in response to an argument you have presented, there is a chance you are being confronted with a weakness in your argument. Perhaps if you had properly defined your terms to begin with, you could have alleviated the confusion with the words chosen, or clarified your use of terms, and in so doing, you could have avoided this frustrating turn of events. In this chapter, we want to discuss some of the ways definitions are essential to making good arguments. We will also provide guidance to know why, when, and how you should define your terms, along with advice on avoiding mistakes in defining terms. In the end, we hope to show that when you properly define your terms, you can avoid misunderstanding and confusion, and you can make your arguments stronger than they otherwise would have been.

Why Define Our Terms?

Defining key terms can help us focus on the important ideas and avoid unnecessary distractions. As we have been saying from the beginning of this book, we present arguments because we want to convince our audience that a particular claim or belief is reasonable and that they ought to accept it as being true. So arguments are supposed to be about ideas. Sometimes in debates about very important matters, however, arguments can get off track and participants can become distracted by the words being used.

In arguments about God's existence, for example, it has become quite common to see discussions devolve into debates about the word *atheism*. Does it mean "the belief that God does not exist"? Or does it simply mean "a lack of a belief in God"? The difference is significant. If it is the first definition, then the word represents a viewpoint that carries some burden of proof—the atheist (just like the theist) should be able to provide good reasons to think that her belief is true. But if atheism is simply a lack of a belief in God, then even rocks and trees are atheists (assuming that neither rocks nor trees have any beliefs about whether God exists), and the word loses all significance in the debate about whether God exists. The question about whether God exists is so important that we need to stay focused *on that question*: Does God exist or not? When faced with a question of such magnitude, the last thing we want is to get into a debate about the meaning of the word *atheism*. We should focus instead on the question of whether or not God exists. So when we are debating God's existence and want to use the word *atheism*, we should first say what we mean when we say *atheism* so that our argument is not taken off track. As we seek to make good arguments, being careful to define our terms appropriately can help us avoid these kinds of unnecessary distractions.

In addition to keeping our arguments on the right track, defining key terms appropriately can help us avoid confusion or misunderstanding on the part of our audience. Some very important words have a variety of commonly accepted meanings. Take the word *Christian*, for example. Depending on who you ask, a Christian could be (a) someone who claims to believe in Jesus Christ; (b) someone who behaves as Jesus behaved; (c) someone who assents to a very specific set of interrelated beliefs about the Bible, God, and humanity; (d) someone who has had a conversion experience at which time they professed faith in Jesus (where the definitions of *conversion* and *faith* are key considerations); or (e) someone who was born in any country that historically has had some kind of significant Christian influence. If we are creating an argument about Christians, which of these definitions we have in mind will make all the difference in the world. Here are some other important terms that have a wide variety of commonly accepted meanings:

democracy	evolution
poverty	sin
liberal	salvation
conservative	liberty
rich	Muslim
poor	Christian
religion	Jewish
science	

For each of these terms, some particular meaning may enter your mind when you first think about the word. But if you stop and consider each term carefully, you will recognize that there are other commonly accepted definitions for each of them. Successfully creating a good argument that uses these words, and others like them, will often hinge on our ability to make sure that our audience understands the words the same way we intend them; and if our audience does not share our definition, our arguments are not likely to be successful, no matter how good they otherwise might be.

Dictionary Definitions

Despite these reasons for why we ought to take care to define key terms appropriately, you might still resist, thinking instead that we can just consult a standard dictionary to resolve such issues. After all, the publishing company who produces the dictionary has invested huge amounts of money, time, and effort to make sure the words listed are defined properly. Why should we try to duplicate that effort? Why not just keep a dictionary handy so that we can respond to concerns about definitions as they arise? Well, dictionaries can sometimes be quite helpful, but we want to offer some words of guidance and caution with regard to when and how to use dictionary definitions.

First, dictionaries present the meanings of words with no attached context. Context is one of the most important factors in communication. It refers to the elements of speech used, such as words, sentences, and phrases. But it can also refer to unspoken elements, such as preexisting beliefs or states of mind. Context is also shaped by what subject matter is under consideration in a discussion. But a dictionary does not take any of that into consideration when it gives us the definition of a word. Of course dictionaries can give us some *clues* about context. For example, the dictionary definition for *bat* will let you know that the meaning of the word depends on whether we are talking about baseball or chiropterology.[1] But when we hear the word *bat*, the dictionary cannot tell us how the person using it intends it to be understood. So it is essential to remember that while dictionaries can provide a broad range of usages of a word, they can never supply the specific context in which the word is being used. Since the meaning of words often depends on how they are used in context, we must proceed with caution when consulting a dictionary.

Also related to the issue of context, dictionaries are not specific enough to adequately address terms as they are used in specialized fields of study. Most fields of study have their own technical language or jargon, a set of terms and commonly accepted ways of using those terms that are unique to that field of study. A famous episode of the 1950s TV show *The Honeymooners* illustrates this point effectively. The two main characters, Ralph Kramden and Ed Norton, are attempting to learn how to golf by reading a book. They read the step-by-step instructions for how to begin the golf swing: "First, step up, plant your feet firmly on the ground, and address the ball." Puzzled by what it means to "address the ball," Ed tries to demonstrate. He steps over to

---

1. The winged mammal commonly called a "bat" is classified as belonging to the biological order *Chiroptera*. Chiropterology, then, is the study of mammals belonging to this order.

the ball, plants his feet firmly, and says, "Hello, ball!"[2] Even if Ed had a dictionary handy, it probably wouldn't have been much help. When you look up *address* in most dictionaries, you won't find anything about golf. This is because dictionaries are designed to give a basic understanding of the most common ways a word is used, but this often falls short of what is needed. As you can imagine, this problem is exacerbated when the topic of discussion is something more important, more complex, or more specialized than golf, such as philosophy, theology, science, or religion—or one of the many subdisciplines within these fields. Even when dictionaries do seem to speak to something in one of those specialized fields of study, they seldom give the full picture of what a word means or how it is used within that field. Since dictionaries are not designed to speak to specialized fields of study or arguments, it is best to avoid thinking of a dictionary definition as the final arbiter of what a word means.

Dictionaries do not define words. Rather, for any word, the dictionary simply tells us what the definition is. The distinction is this: words are defined by those who use them, and then those who publish dictionaries simply convey the meanings that have been given to the words by those who use them. Another way to say this is that dictionaries report how words are used; they don't actually create the definitions. For example, the word *awful* has historically referred to something that was full of awe or worthy of awe; however, when we look up this word in a dictionary today, we typically get a definition that connotes an entirely different meaning based on colloquial usage. When you look at it this way, it becomes clear that no dictionary is ultimately authoritative.[3] While dictionaries can be helpful in discovering the meaning of unfamiliar words, we shouldn't think of them as standing above us, ultimately telling us how to use

> Dictionaries do not define words. Rather, for any word, the dictionary simply tells us what the definition is. The distinction is this: words are defined by those who use them.

2. *The Honeymooners*, episode 3, "The Golfer," October 15, 1955.

3. This is one of the reasons why disputes can never be solved by consulting a dictionary.

words. Instead, we should think of a dictionary as a helpful record of the widely accepted and common ways words are used. A dictionary is good if it accurately conveys the common usage of the words listed.

In our final comments about dictionaries, we offer a bit of advice for students in light of the problems we mentioned above: do not quote or cite *any* standard dictionary when you are writing an academic paper. When your professor reads in your paper something like, "Such-and-such dictionary defines *x* as . . . ," she is likely to view that in much the same way as we would view Ed Norton looking in the dictionary to find out what it means to "address the ball." You may have gotten away with citing a standard dictionary in the earliest stages of your academic pursuits (i.e., junior high or high school), but please let us warn you that on the collegiate level and beyond, professors will find this unacceptable, as it reflects a lazy approach to research and argumentation. Our advice is to leave that practice behind you and move on to more sophisticated levels of analysis. If you are studying a particular topic and you don't know what a particular word means, then you should indeed consult a dictionary—preferably a specialized dictionary written specifically for your field of study. But once you have a good grasp of what the words mean, move on to your analysis and leave the dictionaries behind.

Types of Definitions

Dictionary definitions are of a specific type. They are *descriptive* in that they seek to describe how a word is commonly used or what it means. Sometimes this kind of definition is called an *analytic* definition because it analyzes the meaning of the word. When we give a definition of this type, our goal is to point out the preestablished meaning of a word. If a word has a variety of well-known and commonly accepted meanings, we can give a descriptive definition in order to clarify for our audience which sense of the word we have in mind when we use it. Descriptive definitions can be evaluated in terms of their quality. For example, they can be right or wrong, broad or narrow. If, at the beginning of your argument about God's existence, you define *atheist* as "a religious person who follows the teachings of Jesus," your definition will be incorrect. While there isn't always universal agreement about what "atheism" means, it surely isn't that! If you define *automobile* as "a form of motorized transportation," your definition will be correct, but it will also be far too broad since many other types of vehicles fit that definition.

Descriptive definitions point out the established meaning of a term. But another important kind of definition is commonly used in argumentation: the *stipulative* definition. A stipulative definition is given to attach a new meaning to a word, usually for the purpose of convenience in the discussion. Suppose that you engage in a lengthy argument about how to alleviate poverty. You may find it necessary, for the sake of discussion, to stipulate a definition of the term *low income*. You might say something like, "For the purposes of my argument, a low income household is one whose annual income is below 200 percent of the Federal Poverty Level, as established by the U.S. Department of Health and Human Services, using numbers from the year 2016." When a definition like this is given, it assumes no preestablished meaning at all. Instead, it is offered with a new meaning that applies

> A stipulative definition is given to attach a new meaning to a word, usually for the purpose of convenience in the discussion.

specifically to the context of the argument. Using stipulative definitions like this can help move the discussion along with clarity. It would be quite awkward if you had to repeat "households whose annual income is below . . ." each time you wanted to mention it. It would be much easier and more convenient to just stipulate that the term *low income* has that definition. Unlike descriptive definitions, stipulative definitions cannot be right or wrong, too broad or too narrow. The reason for this is that the speaker is stipulating a new meaning, and this meaning is intended to apply only to the narrow context of that particular discussion or argument.

To Define or Not to Define

With all of this in mind, we are faced with the question of when, or how frequently, we should define our terms. Two extreme positions can be ruled out right away. On the one extreme, it is never helpful to attempt to define every term used, as in the following example:

> By *extreme* we mean that there is a diverse spectrum of views, and the one we are mentioning now can be seen as the most stringent of its kind. By *it* we just intend to refer to the subject under consideration. By *is* we don't mean to imply only present-tense action, but rather . . .

As you can see from this example, defining every term used is never necessary, and it always gets in the way of what we really want to do: talk about ideas. The other extreme would be to say that defining terms is never necessary, and the above discussion has demonstrated why that is not the best position to take.

When deciding whether to define a term, there are three principles to follow. First, define a term if you suspect your audience might not know it, or might not understand it the way you are using it. There is no easy formula for determining exactly when these conditions apply. You just need to know your audience and make adjustments accordingly. If you are speaking to a group of chemists, you probably don't need to define the term *solution* as long as you are using it in a way that the chemists would expect. But if you are talking to a group of people who might be unfamiliar with the way this word is used and want to refer to a homogeneous mixture of two substances, one dissolved into the other, you probably need to mention that this is what you mean when you use the term *solution*. If you are speaking to a group of professional theologians, you probably don't need to define much of the technical theological terminology you are using; but if you are speaking to a more general audience, such definitions might be necessary.

Second, define a term if it has more than one meaning that your audience might assume you intend. For example, we devote several passages in the beginning of this book to defining what we mean by the term *argument*. This is a word that has a variety of commonly accepted meanings, and had we not taken great care to describe which of those meanings we had in mind, you could have been quite confused. Hopefully, because we took the time to define our usage of the word, you are not confused.

Third, define terms that have disputed meanings. You may have picked up on the need for this in our discussion about the definition of the word *atheism*. If you want to use a term that you know has a disputed meaning, it will serve your argument well if you clearly state for your audience which meaning you want to use. That way, even if your audience disagrees with your definition, you can still get on with the business of presenting your argument and making your case. The disputed definition will not be a hindrance to your audience understanding what you want to say.

Avoiding Mistakes in the Way We Use Words

In the process of providing definitions that will contribute to our arguments, we can make several mistakes. Some of these mistakes are tempting, but they will do more harm than good.

Stipulation Encroachment

We have already said that it is sometimes necessary to stipulate a new definition of a word for the sake of clarity or simplicity. However, you should never offer a stipulative definition for a word that already has a clearly established or narrow meaning. For example, you should not attempt to stipulate *television* as "the paranormal ability to see objects at great distances." Similarly, you should not attempt to offer a stipulative definition of a word if there is already a word that is known to have the meaning you intend to convey. For example, if you are talking about international affairs, you would not want to stipulate that *key leader* is "the person in a sovereign state who has been vested with the powers to represent that state in international relations." The reason for this is that we already have a common term with that meaning: *head of state*. So, to put forth *key leader* and stipulate that definition would do little more than cause confusion for your audience. In both prior

> You should never offer a stipulative definition for a word that already has a clearly established or narrow meaning.

examples, the stipulation is encroaching on an established meaning. When you do this, you will cause unnecessary confusion for your audience and thus weaken your argument.

Equivocation

Sometimes words are univocal. That is, there is just one possible meaning for the word. Other words are equivocal. Equivocal words have different meanings, all of which are correctly applied to different contexts and different situations. In our example earlier in the chapter, we pointed out that *bat* is one such word. The fallacy of *equivocation* is an informal logical fallacy that improperly leverages words that have multiple meanings.[4] This fallacy occurs when we are intentionally ambiguous in our use of a word so that we can apply it later in the argument with a different meaning than the first. One clear example of this fallacy is the following:

God is love.

Love is a quaint, old-fashioned notion.

Therefore, God is a quaint, old-fashioned notion.

The formal structure of this argument is valid. That is, if the premises are true, then the conclusion is certainly true. However, this argument makes a mistake in reasoning that is not related to its structure. Namely, the argument equivocates on *love*. In the first premise, it is used in an intentionally ambiguous manner. In the second premise, *love* is given a narrower meaning—one that may or may not be correct but is nevertheless a different meaning than what was in view in the first premise. Because the argument makes this mistake in reasoning, the premises cannot count as good reasons to think that the conclusion is true.

The fallacy of equivocation is sometimes made unintentionally. Because of this, we should be slow to assume that those who make this mistake are intentionally misleading us. Additionally, however, if we want to make good arguments, we must be on guard ourselves, lest we unwittingly make this mistake. To expand our understanding,

---

4. See our discussion of formal and informal logical fallacies in chap. 3.

it will be helpful to look at one additional example of this fallacy, one that is commonly used:

There is a moral law.

Laws imply a lawgiver.

Therefore, there is a moral lawgiver.

The reason that this is an example of the fallacy of equivocation is that the word *law* in the first premise has a different meaning from the word *laws* in the second premise. In the first premise, *law* refers to the structure and operation of the world—like the physical law of gravity or the logical law of the excluded middle. In the second premise, however, the word means something like "a rule of behavior issued by an authority or governing body." In fairness, this argument might not always be an example of the fallacy of equivocation. It could very well be that the person offering it intends for *law* in the first premise to mean exactly the same thing as it means in the second premise. In this case, however, the argument would be committing the fallacy of begging the question. If *moral law* refers to an actual authoritative pronouncement about morality, then there must *necessarily* be a moral lawgiver. But since the argument seeks to establish the existence of such a lawgiver, the argument simply begs the question.[5]

Self-Serving Definitions

Closely related to the fallacy of equivocation (and of begging the question) is the mistake of offering self-serving definitions. A *self-serving definition* is one that is constructed to ensure the argument's success. It is "defining your way to victory." For example, if you are making an argument designed to show that Christian moral behavior is good and righteous, you aren't really accomplishing much if you define *Christian* as "someone who behaves as Jesus behaved" and then define *good* behavior as "behavior similar to Jesus's behavior." If you give these self-serving definitions, all you have done is define Christian moral behavior as good. You haven't really made a case

5. As a practical exercise, think of ways in which this sample argument might be improved so that it avoids both equivocation and the fallacy of begging the question.

that it is good. So if you want to make a good argument, you should avoid giving self-serving definitions.

Circular Definitions

Circular definitions are ones that don't really explain the meaning of the word. For example, if we define *straight* as "the shape of a path a person takes when walking in a straight line," this doesn't *really* tell us what *straight* means. If we define *republican* as "a person who advocates a republican form of government," or *quickly* as "having the quality of quickness," we haven't said much. One of the hallmarks of a circular definition is that it uses the word it seeks to define in the definition (although this is not always the case). If you take the time to define an important term, you should avoid circular definitions at all costs. The goal in providing a definition is to increase clarity so your audience understands what you mean when you use specific words in your argument. If you want to make a good argument, avoid circular definitions for your terms.

Conclusion

We hope it is evident that defining your terms is a necessary part of argumentation, especially when you use words or ideas that could have confusing or multiple meanings. Without investing in this foundational task, you run the risk that your argument will be misunderstood, and if it is misunderstood, it can never be effective. We argue because we believe we have something important to say. Since this is the case, we must make sure we say it in such a way that removes the potential for miscommunication. Defining your terms will help you to alleviate this potential pitfall and will give greater clarity, substance, and effectiveness to your argument.

6

Drawing Analogies

Properly employed, analogies can be powerful tools for communication. Analogies compare two things that are alike in some relevant respect. When properly constructed, an analogy can leverage the audience's preexisting knowledge of one item of comparison to expand knowledge and understanding of the other. Additionally, analogies can help construct good arguments that lead the audience to adopt the conclusion.

Simple Analogies

An *analogy* is a comparison between two different items, drawing on a relevant feature of one item in order to better understand the other. Often, metaphors and similes (both figures of speech) are used in order to convey the analogy. For example, in the 1994 movie of the same name, Forrest Gump famously quipped, "Life is like a box of chocolates. You never know what you are going to get."[1] This is an example of a simple analogy, using a simile to make the comparison. Traditional boxes of chocolate-covered candies contain an assortment

1. *Forrest Gump*, directed by Robert Zemerckis (Paramount, 1994). In this scene Forrest Gump, played by Tom Hanks, is actually reporting something his mother always told him.

of varieties. So when you select a piece, you don't know what you have until you take a bite. This "variety with surprise" feature of the chocolate is what Forrest wants to draw on to better understand what life is like: full of a variety of experiences that can't really be predicted. In this simple analogy, two things are compared for the purpose of drawing on a feature of one item and relating it to the other.

As we noted above, simple analogies are communicated most often using either simile or metaphor. Similes and metaphors are figures of speech used to make the comparison and draw out the analogy.

> An analogy is a comparison between two different items for the purpose of drawing on a relevant feature of one item in order to better understand the other.

Metaphors are usually thought of as comparisons without an explicit explanation of the comparison. The old adage "Don't burn your bridges" makes use of metaphor. While not explicitly stated, the two items being compared are "potentially useful relationships" and "bridges." The admonition is that one should not alienate people or damage relationships that may prove useful or beneficial in the future, just as one should not burn a bridge that might later be needed to cross a body of water. Here are some famous analogies made by metaphor that you might recognize:

- "I am the good shepherd. I know my own and my own know me, just as the Father knows me and I know the Father; and I lay down my life for the sheep."—Jesus[2]
- "All the world's a stage, / And all the men and women merely players."—William Shakespeare[3]
- "Life's a dance."—John Michael Montgomery[4]
- "Hope is the thing with feathers / That perches in the soul."—Emily Dickinson[5]

2. John 10:14–15.
3. William Shakespeare, *As You Like It*, act 2, scene 4.
4. John Michael Montgomery, "Life's a Dance," by Allen Shamblin and Steve Seskin (*Atlantic*, 1992).
5. Emily Dickinson, "'Hope' Is the Thing with Feathers," lines 1–2.

The Forrest Gump example mentioned above is a simile—it provides the comparison and states it explicitly: "Life is like a box of chocolates." The "Don't burn your bridges" metaphor could also be stated as a simile: "Relationships are like bridges: you shouldn't burn them down in case you need them in the future."

As these examples show, analogies can be quite useful in the course of regular communication. One of the most obvious benefits of using analogies is that they can *replace* long explanations (like the one about bridges in the preceding paragraph). Good analogies are short, communicate much information, and are obvious to the audience, making longer explanations unnecessary. Another benefit to using an analogy is that it can help an audience learn about something unfamiliar by comparing it to something well known. Analogies can also be helpful when an audience is being introduced to complex concepts in specialized fields, such as when various functions of a simple cell in biology are compared to man-made machines. Simple analogies, then, help us explain or illustrate the ideas we wish to convey.

Arguments by Analogy

So far we've only mentioned analogies in the context of efforts to simply communicate information. But communicating information by means of analogy is not an argument. However, arguments can be made that make use of analogy in order to persuade the audience to adopt the conclusion. *Arguments by analogy* suggest that because the two items being compared are alike in one respect, they are also alike in some other respect. The basic structure of a common argument by analogy is as follows:

Objects x and y have properties $P1$, $P2$, and $P3$.

Object x has property $P4$.

Therefore, y probably also has property $P4$.

You might notice that this structure resembles those examples of inductive reasoning we mentioned in an earlier chapter, and indeed *most arguments by analogy are inductive arguments*. Recall that inductive reasoning involves collecting observed evidence that points to a probable conclusion. Arguments by analogy usually make this same move: they use the observed similarities between the items being compared as the basis for concluding that the items probably have further similarities that are not observed.

One very famous argument by analogy that shares these features is William Paley's "watchmaker argument," a kind of teleological argument for God's existence. Paley pointed out that if you were out for a walk one day in a field and you found a watch lying on the ground, you would quickly conclude that someone made the watch. Paley says this is so because you would recognize the design-like features of the watch (for example, the fact that it is an ordered system of complex parts, working together to display the time of day). Of course you would be correct that the watch has a designer: you can verify independently that the watch was designed and built by someone. Paley then points to the design-like features in the natural world. The analogy, then, is this: Both the watch and the natural world have design-like features. In the watch, the design-like features arise because it was designed by an intelligent designer. Therefore, the design-like features of the natural world probably arise because the natural world was designed by an intelligent designer.

> Arguments by analogy suggest that because the two items being compared are alike in one respect, they are also alike in some other respect.

Recall one key difference between inductive and deductive reasoning: in a valid deductive argument, if the premises are true, the conclusion is certainly true. This is because the premises logically entail the conclusion. Therefore, deductive arguments are an all-or-nothing affair. They cannot be made stronger or weaker. Inductive arguments, on the other hand, have premises that do not entail the conclusion but rather work together to show that the conclusion is probably true. So, inductive arguments can be strong or weak, and weak arguments can be made stronger by adding more evidence. The same can be said of inductive arguments by analogy, and it is helpful to consider factors that may make arguments by analogy stronger or weaker.

Number of Similarities

Considering the example structure above, it might be possible to increase our confidence in the conclusion if we observe an increase in the number of observed shared properties. If x and y also share properties $P5$, $P6$, and $P7$, this might lead us to be even more confident that y has $P4$ as well. For example, let's say that three friends purchase a particular make of car, and they are happy with it. Using an argument by analogy, I could conclude that if I purchase that same make of car, I will be happy with it as well. However, if those three friends purchase the same exact model of car, with the same engine specifications and same interior configuration, and each of those three friends shares the same taste in cars that I have—then the argument by analogy is much stronger. I can be even more confident that if I purchase that exact model and configuration, I will be happy with it as well. Notice that the similarities in this example are higher in number and diverse in kind (many features of the car itself and shared taste in cars among the friends). Arguments by analogy are stronger

Deductive arguments are an all-or-nothing affair. They cannot be made stronger or weaker. Inductive arguments, on the other hand, have premises that do not entail the conclusion but rather work together to show that the conclusion is probably true.

with a higher number of diverse similarities shared by the objects being compared, and they are weaker if there are few similarities.

Number of Objects

Arguments by analogy are also stronger when a larger number of objects are compared. If just one of my friends purchases a new car and is happy with it, I can have some amount of confidence that I will be happy if I purchase the same kind of car. If I observe the same happiness resulting from the same kind of car among three or four friends, however, I am even more confident that the same kind of car will also make me happy. Or suppose that a medical researcher is attempting to determine whether a new drug has a particular side effect. The researcher doesn't know exactly what the drug is doing inside the body, so she must rely on analogy: Does the same drug produce the same side effects in the patient? A higher number of patients who both take the drug and experience the side effect, combined with a higher number of patients who do not take the drug and do not experience the side effect, would increase the researcher's confidence in the conclusion. If, on the other hand, the researcher only has a few patients to observe, the analogy will be weak.

Modesty of Conclusion Relative to Premises

All inductive arguments involve a leap of some distance from the observed to conclusions about the unobserved. In an inductive argument by analogy, the more modest the claim made by the conclusion, the smaller the leap we are being asked to make, and the more confident we can be. Let's say that my four friends and I each purchase the exact same make and model of car with the exact same features and configuration. If each of my friends is able to get 30 mpg fuel economy, it is probably safer to conclude that I will get *up to* 30 mpg than to conclude that I will get *at least* 30 mpg. In this example, up to 30 mpg is a more modest conclusion relative to the evidence presented in the analogy. This makes the argument stronger, and we can have more confidence that the conclusion is true. The bolder the conclusion is relative to the evidence in the premises, on the other hand, the weaker the argument is, and the less confidence we can have in the conclusion.

Relevance of Similarities to the Conclusion

Arguments by analogy are also weak if the similarities shared between the items being compared are not relevant to the conclusion. Hockey players are sometimes known to be "superstitious," and sometimes superstition is merely an argument by analogy in which the similarities are not relevant to the conclusion. For example, let's say that a hockey player suffers through a long scoring drought but then scores a goal in ten games straight. The difference was that before each of those ten, he put on his left skate before he put on his right skate. He might then draw the conclusion that if he puts his left skate on before his right in the next game, he will also score a goal in that game. The similarity that this hockey player points to in comparing those games is the order in which he puts his skates on: left then right. But is this similarity relevant to the conclusion? Hardly. One factor that *could* be relevant is that the opposing teams' goalies faced during the scoring drought were more highly skilled, while the goalies faced in the latter games were not as highly skilled. The skill of the opposing team's goalie surely is relevant; the order in which the player gets dressed is not. Arguments by analogy are stronger if the similarities are relevant to the conclusion.

Presence of Dissimilarities

The greater number of diverse similarities, the stronger the analogy; but if there are relevant dissimilarities, then the analogy is weaker. Let's say that you have enjoyed all six Star Wars movies released prior to 2015, episodes 1–6. In fact, you think they are the best movies you have ever seen. By analogy, you could say that because you enjoyed the first six episodes, you will enjoy watching the newest Star Wars movies, episodes 7–9. However, an important dissimilarity may weaken the analogy: George Lucas wrote episodes 1–6; but J. J. Abrams wrote episode 7, and Rian Johnson wrote episodes 8 and 9. If you liked the first six episodes *because you like movies written by George Lucas*, then just because the new movies are part of the Star Wars franchise does not indicate that you will enjoy them. The difference in who wrote the movies is a relevant dissimilarity that weakens the argument. On the other hand, if you enjoyed the movies because of the general storyline or themes, then the dissimilarity might not be relevant to the argument.

The Fallacy of the False Analogy

Some analogies have such glaring dissimilarities and obviously irrelevant similarities that we call them "false analogies." Arguments based on false analogies are fallacious. One example from a recent public policy debate involves mandatory health insurance:

> Requiring people to purchase car insurance is a good thing.
> Health insurance and car insurance are both types of insurance.
> Therefore, it is also good to require people to purchase health insurance.

While the conclusion may indeed be true, the argument is based on a false analogy and is therefore fallacious. In this example, there are (at least) two glaring dissimilarities between the items being compared. First, unlike the proposal for health insurance, car insurance is not universally required. It is only required for those people who operate cars on public roads. If a person does not wish to purchase car insurance, he or she does not have to. There are many other transportation options, and many people live in cities where owning a car is far from a necessity. These people are not required to purchase car insurance. Second, the kind of insurance required for people who operate cars on public roads is liability insurance: it provides for financial payments to those who may be harmed by the illegal or unintentional actions of the driver. The owner of the policy does not receive financial benefit from this kind of insurance, and indeed the owner hopes that the insurance is never needed. This is quite unlike health insurance, which always benefits the owner of the policy and is expected to be used on a regular basis. These (and perhaps other) glaring dissimilarities make the analogy a false one. There may be other reasons to think that it is good to require people to purchase health insurance, but this particular argument is fallacious and therefore cannot support the conclusion.

Conclusion

The number of similarities, the number of objects, the modesty of the conclusion in relation to the premises, the relevance of similarities in relation to the conclusion, and the presence of dissimilarities are all factors that can be used to evaluate arguments by analogy. We can learn to analyze analogies to see whether there is a sufficient number of relevant similarities, or a sufficient number of objects of comparison; we can consider whether the conclusion is modest or whether it is too bold, given the premises; and we can observe whether the similarities are relevant to the conclusion. Learning how to evaluate arguments by analogy will help us in two distinct respects. First, it will help us evaluate the arguments by analogy that are offered by others so we can determine whether the proposed conclusions to these arguments are true or false. When we encounter a strong argument by analogy, perhaps we should have confidence that the conclusion is true. Second, learning how to evaluate arguments by analogy can better equip us to make arguments of our own that are based on analogy. Using these criteria can help us craft good arguments that are likely to convince our audience that our claim is true.

7

Cause and Effect

It is undeniable that an increase in illness during flu season is accompanied by a dramatic increase in visits to doctors' offices. Therefore, we can conclude that visiting the doctor's office causes the flu . . . or can we? The kind of reasoning we need in order to analyze the relationship between events such as these is *causal reasoning*—reasoning about cause-and-effect relationships between observed events. If we want to make a good causal argument (for example, an argument about what causes the flu), knowing how to properly engage in causal reasoning is essential. In this chapter we present a brief overview of causal reasoning, including important factors to consider when developing causal arguments.

Basic Causal Reasoning

Consider the examples shown below, each stated in the form of a question. In each case, the question can be answered by employing cause-and-effect reasoning.

- Does Vitamin C prevent the common cold?
- Why don't more people vote?

- Will the tax increase result in the desired outcome?
- Why are certain minority groups arrested and incarcerated at higher per capita rates?
- Do seatbelts decrease car accident injuries?
- Why do some church denominations increase in membership while others decrease?
- Is gender bias to blame for lower pay rates among female workers?
- Why is the unemployment rate high?
- Has the "war on drugs" helped decrease drug use?

If we genuinely want to know the answer to questions like these, we begin the process of causal reasoning either to determine the causes of the effects we see or to predict the effects of proposed causes.

When we begin with the effect, this kind of reasoning is an effort to understand how it came about that something happened: why it happened, how it happened, or who or what made it happen. We first observe the effect, and then we reason about what caused it. Taking advantage of reasoning to the cause from the effect is a common part of plots in novels, television shows, and movies. An episode of a show about solving crimes, for example, will begin with the crime committed, and the rest of the program is devoted to the detectives solving the crime and discovering the guilty person and how he or she did it. This might be the most intuitive and easy to understand form of causal reasoning.

While reasoning from the effect to a cause is common, causal reasoning works the other direction as well. Sometimes causal reasoning begins with the cause and works toward the effect. In these cases, we engage in causal reasoning in an effort to understand what effects a particular cause may bring about. Being able to do this can help us prevent or avoid negative consequences of certain actions. If we see a child reaching toward a hot pan on the stove top, we may reason very quickly that this action will produce the effect of harming the child, and then we take action to stop it. When driving home from work, I may quickly reason that taking the highway will result in my being stuck in traffic. So I decide to take back roads instead. Of course the same kind of reasoning that helps us avoid undesirable consequences can help us achieve desirable consequences: we can reason among various courses of action and choose to take the one that will have the most desirable effect.

Correlations and Inductive Reasoning

Cause-and-effect reasoning often begins with what is called *correlation*: regularly associating two events with one another. When one happens, the other happens also. Every time it rains, water appears in the basement. Every Tuesday at three o'clock, the red truck drives by. Every time I bend my elbow, pain shoots up my arm. People who pray more often tend to report a deeper sense of connection to God. Each of these is an example of correlation—one event is always observed to follow or be connected with another. Human beings have the built-in rational ability to notice these close associations and to begin to make connections between events that are closely associated. It is quite natural that once we see these associations, we begin to explore the idea of whether one of these events causes the other.

Philosopher David Hume (1711–76) referred to correlation as "the constant conjunction" between one event and another. In one important passage in *An Enquiry Concerning Human Understanding*, Hume explains how we begin to move from correlation to causation. He writes, "In all single instances . . . there is nothing that produces any impression, nor consequently can suggest any idea of power or necessary connection [of causation]. But when many uniform instances appear, and the same object is always followed by the same event, we then begin to entertain the notion of cause and connection."[1] In other words, Hume is pointing out that if it just so happens on one occasion that

> Cause-and-effect reasoning often begins with what is called *correlation*: regularly associating two events with one another. When one happens, the other happens also.

1. David Hume, *An Enquiry Concerning Human Understanding*, 7.2. Quotations are from David Hume, *An Enquiry Concerning Human Understanding with a Letter*

two events appear together, nothing about that would lead us to infer causation from one to the other. However, when we constantly see the same two events, and one always follows the other, it is then that we begin to think there is a "necessary connection" of causation between them—that one causes the other.

Perhaps you can see that this sort of reasoning is inductive.[2] Recall that inductive reasoning depends on the accumulation of evidence that points to a probable conclusion. In cause-and-effect reasoning from correlation, the correlation acts as evidence suggesting the probability of causation. The more evidence we have—that is, the greater number of occasions that we observe the correlation—the better reason we have to conclude that the correlation is indication of causation. Moreover, when we are confident that one event causes the other, we can begin to make predictions about what will happen in the future when the *cause* happens: we predict that it will bring about the closely associated event, or the *effect*.

Hume also introduced into this discussion a problem that may give us reason to be skeptical about inductive cause-and-effect reasoning. We can begin to see the problem when we ask, what exactly is the power of causation? Hume writes, "After [a person] has observed several instances of [correlation], he then pronounces them to be connected [as cause and effect]. What alteration has happened to give rise to this new idea of connection? Nothing but how he feels these events to be connected in his imagination, and he can readily foretell the existence of one from the appearance of the other."[3] What Hume points out here is the difficulty we have seeing the power that one event has to cause another. It is easy to see that one event always precedes another. But it is difficult to make the transition from "always precedes" to "causes," especially when we can't see precisely what it is about the one that could cause the other. Thus, while we cannot dogmatically claim that correlation is equal to causation, we can argue inductively, using observed correlations as possible evidence for causation.

---

from a Gentleman to His Friend in Edinburgh and Hume's Abstract of a Treatise of Human Nature, ed. Eric Steinberg, 2nd ed. (Indianapolis: Hackett, 1993), 52.

2. We discussed inductive reasoning in chap. 2.

3. Hume, *Enquiry*, 7.2, p. 50.

The Post Hoc, Ergo Propter Hoc *Fallacy*

In pointing out the difficulty of understanding causation and Hume's comments about it, we aren't advocating skepticism or lack of confidence in inductive cause-and-effect reasoning. Rather, we are simply applying a weakness inherent in inductive reasoning to inductive cause-and-effect reasoning: we can never be 100 percent certain of the conclusion. This leads us directly to one potential fallacy we may inadvertently commit when we engage in causal reasoning. The fallacy is called *post hoc, ergo propter hoc*, which is Latin for "after this, therefore because of this." This is the mistaken assumption that simply because the second event comes after the first event, the first event caused the second event. In other words, it mistakes a before-and-after relationship for a cause-and-effect relationship between two events. This mistake in reasoning can be especially tempting in cases in which the second event seems to *always* follow from the first.

A falling barometer, for example, almost always precedes an undesirable change in the weather, such as a storm. If every time we observe the falling barometer we also observe a storm after that, should we conclude that the falling barometer causes the storm? Of course not. In this case, both the falling barometer and the storm are effects brought about by the same cause, and that explains why we see the storm after the falling barometer. But it is important to remember that a before-and-after relationship does not necessarily imply a cause-and-effect relationship.

> Post hoc, ergo propter hoc is the mistaken assumption that simply because the second event comes after the first event, the first event caused the second event.

Relevant Differences and Common Threads

Figuring out whether a correlation is a case of cause and effect is never foolproof, but there are some important ways of thinking that can help. When looking at specific cases or examples in which we are looking for a cause, we can look at *relevant differences* and *relevant common threads*. If we are accustomed to thinking that things work out a certain way in a certain situation, and then— unexpectedly—things don't work out that way, we look for a cause. Every year you plant tomatoes in the garden, and every year you end up with a wimpy crop of withered vines that produce a meager number of small, malformed tomatoes. But this year you plant them and are surprised to see a bumper crop of healthy, delicious, bright red tomatoes. What was the difference? There may be many things that are different. It could be that this is the first year that the Jones family lived next door. Perhaps your favorite football team won the championship this year too. But whether the Jones family lives next door or your favorite team won the championship are not relevant differences as it concerns the tomatoes. Perhaps, however, you also decided to switch to a new brand of fertilizer this year. Fertilizer (whether it is used, which brand or type is used, etc.) certainly is a relevant factor when it comes to growing tomatoes. If the only *relevant* difference between this year and all the other years is that you decided to use a new brand of fertilizer, then you have good reason to believe that the fertilizer is the cause of the change in the tomato crop. We've made this example easy to see, but the principle remains the same even for complex, more obscure cases.

In addition to looking at relevant differences, it is also helpful to look for relevant common threads. When there are multiple occurrences of an observed effect, and one relevant common thread is observed among these occurrences, then we have good reason to think that the relevant common thread is the cause. Perhaps during a conference, a sizable group of attendees becomes ill one afternoon. What could be the cause of this? Looking at common threads can help you discover the likely cause. Of course each person who became ill is in attendance at the conference, and each of them (let's say) is over twenty-five years of age. Let's also say that all of those who became ill are men. These are all common threads, but attendance at a conference, age, and gender are not necessarily relevant to the fact that they became ill. It would be fairly easy to discover that all of those who became ill ate at the same restaurant for lunch. Since a lunch meal can be relevant to becoming ill after the meal is consumed, this is a relevant factor, and it gives us good reason to consider the restaurant as the source of the illness (as opposed to age or gender).

Let's also say that all the men who became ill ate at the buffet; other men ate at the same restaurant but did not eat at the buffet and did not become ill. We seem to have found our cause. Eating at the buffet is the only relevant common thread among those who became ill, so we have good reason to think that the buffet was the cause.

Chains and Clusters of Causation

So far the examples we have offered are fairly simple and straightforward: one effect from one cause. But cause-and-effect relationships are not always that simple. Sometimes instead of one cause resulting in one effect, a series of effects become causes of other effects, which bring about other effects, in a long chain of cause and effect. When a person becomes infected with malaria after a mosquito bite, for example, the mosquito bite is simply the final cause in a causal chain: first, an infected person is bitten by a mosquito; then the protozoa multiply in that mosquito; then the mosquito bites an uninfected person, who then becomes infected. When considering causal chains, we see that there are *immediate* causes and *remote* causes. The immediate cause in a causal chain is that which occurs just prior to the effect and is sometimes the most obvious. In the example of a person becoming infected with malaria, the immediate cause is the mosquito host biting the person. Remote causes are those that occur further away from the final effect in the causal chain and are sometimes not as obvious. In the malaria example, the mosquito first biting the person who is already infected is a remote cause.

> Cause-and-effect relationships are not always that simple. Sometimes instead of one cause resulting in one effect, a series of effects become causes of other effects, which bring about other effects, in a long chain of cause and effect.

In addition to chains, sometimes causes contribute to effects in "clusters." A cluster of causation is one in which there are various contributing causes to an effect that may not be related to one another. When a highly favored football team loses a game against an inferior opposing team, analysts will likely be able to identify many causes that contributed to the unexpected outcome. Perhaps a skilled player on the favored team was playing with a minor injury that affected his performance, or perhaps a group of players made a significant mistake on a key play. Perhaps the officials made a bad call, or perhaps the star quarterback was not able to play because of an injury. In situations such as these, it isn't possible to point to one singular cause. Perhaps in a situation such as this, a *main cause* can be identified (such as the absence of the star quarterback). But even though that may be the main cause, the others are still *contributing causes*, because they too had an effect on the outcome of the game.

> The immediate cause in a causal chain is that which occurs just prior to the effect and is sometimes the most obvious. Remote causes are those that occur further away from the final effect in the causal chain and are sometimes not as obvious.

Avoiding Mistakes in Causal Reasoning

Employing these features of basic causal reasoning (relevant differences, common threads, chains and clusters of cause and effect) can help us make good arguments, but there is also the potential that we will make mistakes. To make a good causal argument, we must be aware of these potential mistakes so that we can avoid them. We have already identified the *post hoc* fallacy above; here we will briefly mention three others.

One common mistake is *reversing* cause and effect: the effect is observed and assumed to be the cause, and the cause is assumed to be the effect. In some situations it would be difficult to see how anyone could make this mistake: it isn't likely that someone would say that severe pain caused a broken bone. However, it might be tempting to say that depictions of immorality on television and in movies cause a general decline in morality in the culture. Why might this be a mistake? Movies and television programs are generally a reflection of culture, displaying the values that are held by a majority of people in the culture. So it could very well be that the general decline in moral values in the culture is what causes depictions of immorality on television and in movies. It is also possible that the relationship between moral values in the culture at large and the moral values depicted in visual arts goes in both directions.

Sometimes when two events are observed, we mistakenly believe that one causes the other when they actually share a *common cause*. It is observed, for example, that cities with a higher church attendance on Sunday also have higher numbers of traffic accidents. Should we conclude that higher church attendance is the cause of the higher number of traffic accidents? Probably not. In this case, it is much more likely that both high church attendance and a high number of traffic accidents share a common underlying cause: a higher overall population, with both church attendance and traffic accidents occurring at per capita rates similar to other cities. It would be a mistake, in correlations such as this, to try to treat one event as causing the other when they both actually share a common underlying cause.

In some instances there is no connection between the two events that are observed; thus the correlation is purely *coincidental*. Our superstitious hockey player from chapter 6 might observe a correlation between which skate he puts on first and whether he scores a goal or whether his team wins the game. Obviously (to everyone else, at least) it would be a mistake in reasoning to think that the order in which the skates were put on actually has a causal relationship to the goal being scored or the team winning the game. Even if a strong correlation is observed—that is, even if it is true that *every time* he puts the left skate on first, he scores a goal—it is plain that there is no causal connection between the two. The correlation is just a coincidence. It would be a mistake to assume that there is a causal connection or that both are the effects of the same underlying cause when they do not share this kind of relationship.

Making a Causal Argument

Taking all of this into consideration moves us in the right direction: toward developing a good causal argument. From the above principles of causal reasoning, we can arrive at five practical steps for making causal arguments.

1. Establish the Need

The best causal arguments will most likely be lost on your audience unless they first understand why it is important to discover the cause of the effect that has been observed, or why it is important to predict accurately the effects that certain events may have caused. If you explain negative or positive effects in a way that is relevant to your audience, they may be more interested in the relationship between the cause and these effects. If you can show that a desired outcome can be achieved, your audience may be eager to know which cause will accomplish this outcome.

2. Show Clear Reasoning

If a strong correlation is observed, start there. Then show why you have good grounds to think there is also a cause-and-effect relationship. If your argument depends on observing relevant differences or relevant common threads, state them clearly. If you are pointing to an effect at the end of a chain of causation, include both remote and immediate causes in your explanation. If there are many contributing factors, make that clear also; and leave plenty of room for contributing causes that you may not have discovered.

3. Rule Out Possible Mistakes

Sometimes it is assumed that acknowledging possible mistakes makes an argument weaker. Rest assured that an antagonistic audience is already on the lookout for mistakes in reasoning, so it can only serve to strengthen your position if you make it clear that you have examined your own reasoning for possible mistakes. This is perhaps especially true in causal arguments because causal relationships can be complex and difficult to explain accurately. After you have shown your reasoning, take it a step further and explain why you are confident that you haven't committed the *post hoc, ergo propter hoc* fallacy, for example. Explain why you are sure you haven't reversed cause and effect, or how likely it is that you have overlooked a common underlying cause. Make sure you give serious thought to the idea that there is only a coincidental relationship that accompanies the correlation you observed.

4. Seriously Consider the Alternatives

Once you have laid out your reasoning and given your audience good reason to think that you have avoided mistakes, you should also consider alternative explanations. Since an effect can have any number of causes, you need to make sure that you take seriously proposals suggesting causes different from those you think brought about the effect. If other causes have been suggested, carefully show that they are not capable of producing the effect, or explain what factors help you to know that they haven't done so in this case. The more thorough you are in considering positions that do not agree with your own, the more confident your audience will be that you have explained the causal relationship properly.

5. Avoid Overconfidence

Remember that in most cases your causal arguments rely on inductive reasoning. Unlike deductive reasoning, inductive reasoning can only lead us to a probable conclusion or a likely explanation. It can never lead us to 100 percent certainty. It may also be important to remember Hume's cautionary comments about how we connect two events in our minds in order to see a cause-and-effect relationship. As sure as we are that this cause brought about that effect, we can be wrong. Since we can be wrong, causal arguments (and other kinds too), even very strong ones, should include a healthy dose of humility.

Conclusion

Visits to the doctor's office do not cause the flu, and a falling barometer does not cause the change in weather. These examples might be easy to see, but it is often much more difficult to know when we are justified in arguing causation from observed correlation. Even when we are justified in making the case for causation from correlation, many mistakes can be made along the way. We hope you have gained insight from this chapter about how to determine whether a correlation is an example of cause and effect and about how to properly use inductive reasoning to make the case for causation. We also hope you recognize that reasoning about cause and effect, as with other kinds of induction, never leads to 100 percent certainty. There will always be room for your conclusion to be false, no matter how strong a case you have made. Do not let this keep you from making your arguments about cause and effect, but let it spur you on with caution (and confidence) as you examine the correlations you are observing in order to make your causal arguments.

8

On Good Authority

No one knows everything . . . you included. It stands to reason, then, that if you want to make good arguments, you will need to rely on the arguments, ideas, and expertise of other authors. Even if you are able to make a good argument entirely on your own, you can always strengthen your position and bolster your case when you rely on the work of the experts who have come before you. In this chapter we want to help you understand how to find and use high-quality experts and other sources of authority as support in your arguments.

There are different reasons you might want to consult an authoritative source as you craft your argument. For example, you might want to cite a source that provides certain kinds of factual information or data that helps inform your ideas. A pollster can tell you how many people in a given region support a presidential candidate. Sociologists can tell you what the largest religious group is in a particular country. A historian can tell you when an important event occurred. This kind of factual data might be essential as you make your case, so citing these kinds of authoritative sources can be helpful.

You might also want to cite an expert who has developed an argument for one of your premises. When you are making your argument, the truth of the conclusion depends on the truth of the premises. Perhaps one or more of your premises are not obviously true (which is often the case). If another person has developed an air-tight argument for the truth of one of your premises, then you can cite that argument without having to repeat that work. You can focus on your argument and how your premises lead to your conclusion.

Another reason to cite an authoritative source would be if a scholar has given an expert opinion about a complex subject or a field in which not many people have expertise. This is especially true if you are working in one field (say, philosophy), and part of your argument appeals to a specialized field in neuroscience. You might feel confident in the philosophical work, but citing the expert for her analysis in neuroscience can help fill in your lack of expertise.

You can likely think of beneficial reasons to cite authoritative sources other than the ones mentioned here. But before we move on to guidance for finding and using good sources, we want to discuss two poor reasons students have for quoting a particular source. First, you might be tempted to quote someone simply because you really like what they have to say. Certain writers have an eloquence about them that tends to be emotionally persuasive. There isn't necessarily anything wrong with quoting something "inspirational"; you just need to keep in mind that eloquence, or the ability to evoke an emotional response, cannot (by itself) help strengthen an argument. You might inspire people, but when the inspiration wears off, the audience will be thinking about the weaknesses in the argument rather than the emotion of the quotation. Second, you might be tempted to simply reproduce what another author has said about a topic. Remember that in most contexts your audience will expect that you have conducted your own original analysis of the topic, following your own structure and making your own argument. When you do this, you can support your analysis by quoting and citing authoritative scholarly sources. The important distinction here is between using sources to support your own original analysis (which is what you should do) and using them to provide the actual substance of your argument (which is what you should not do). Remember that your audience has the ability to read those other authors just as much as you do. There is no need to simply report what others have said unless doing so is critical to provide authoritative support to your own original analysis as you work to develop a good argument.

Finding Good Sources

As you do research in the development of an argument, you should take care to focus only on high-quality sources. There are several obvious benefits to doing so. First, when you find and use high-quality sources, you can be confident that the factual information you get from those sources is correct. Second, these sources will teach you something about the topic you are researching so you will be better equipped to make good arguments and assertions about your topic. Third, when you use only high-quality sources, your research is more likely to be balanced, and less likely to be one-sided. Poor-quality sources are often drastically one-sided in their consideration of various topics and ideas, but good-quality sources will be more likely to consider all aspects. Finally, when you use good-quality sources in your research, your audience will see that you have done your homework and as a result will be more likely to take your arguments seriously. So you know you need to focus on high-quality sources . . . but what exactly is "high quality"? The three most important things to look for are recognized expertise, scholarly publication, and current information.

Recognized Expertise

When you are relying on another person to speak to a specific issue, it is essential that that person be a recognized expert on that issue. If you want to make a point about a scientific issue, consult a professionally trained scientist. If you are addressing the finer points of automotive repair, consult a professional mechanic. Addressing a matter of theology? Turn to a theologian. Discussing the climate? Look for a climatologist. The topic or issue that you want to address in your argument will determine the kind of expert sources that are good. However, if you are the only one who thinks that the source is an expert, that will usually not be enough. When you quote someone, the person's expertise should be well recognized and commonly accepted. A scientist who holds a prestigious position in her field at a major university is a recognized expert, while someone who just happens to have a degree in science probably isn't. Admittedly, figuring out who is recognized can be difficult, but there are certain criteria you can look for that will increase your confidence: published authors, those who actively work in their field, and those who teach others in their field all tend to be reliable experts. Given the large number of people throughout the world who are interested in a certain topic, those who are experts form a very small segment of this population. Experts are a select group of people who have given their life to the study of a certain topic. Relying on these kinds of recognized experts will help you make better arguments—arguments that will likely have a better return on your investment.

It should go without saying that not all experts will be helpful to your argument, but only those who have *relevant* expertise. Recall from chapter 3 that appealing to an authority figure for an issue outside her expertise can be fallacious and thus cannot do much to help the argument. A good example of this comes from Ben's background. As a new seminary student transitioning from an undergraduate degree, Ben needed to write a paper on Pauline theology for his first-year New Testament course. Throughout the paper, Ben cited one of his brilliant mentors. After all, his mentor had a PhD and was a professor at his alma mater. The problem was that his mentor's PhD was in chemistry and not New Testament or theology. The feedback from his seminary professor read, "Who is this source? I don't recognize him!" The reason Ben's professor didn't recognize Ben's mentor is that he wasn't an expert in the relevant field of study. So, if you are addressing a matter of philosophy or theology, a scientist is the wrong person to consult. If you are addressing a matter of electrical repair, a plumber is probably not the right person to consult. It is essential that you consult experts whose expertise pertains clearly to the topic addressed in your argument.

But even in cases in which the person is a legitimate expert in the topic under consideration, the expertise the person has might not be the most relevant. If you are shopping for a refrigerator, someone who repairs refrigerators for a living certainly has the technical qualifications and appropriate expertise to tell you some details about refrigerators. However, the expertise of the salesperson might be more relevant to your decision. If the salesperson's commission depends (as it often does in today's marketplace) on the customer being happy and keeping the new refrigerator (as opposed to returning it), then the salesperson will quickly become an expert on which makes and models of refrigerators result in the highest rates of customer satisfaction. Even though both the repairman and the salesperson are experts, expertise in the area of customer satisfaction may be *more relevant* when deciding on which refrigerator to purchase. So it is important to remember that even if someone is an expert in the broad topic you are considering, you may still need to do more work to find out which expert can provide the most relevant contribution to your argument.

Scholarly Publication

In addition to recognized expertise, it is important to use sources that are credible and reliable, and the most credible and reliable sources will be found in scholarly publications. Scholarly publications tend to be more reliable because they are peer reviewed. Peer reviewing is the process by which an author's work is first reviewed by other recognized experts in the field, who examine the work to make sure it meets commonly accepted standards for scholarly work in that field. If an author submits a paper to an academic journal, for example, the editors will send copies of that paper to several scholars who act as "referees" and comment on the quality of the work. This is usually done with the author's name or other identifying information removed, in order to prevent potential bias based on the name recognition of the author. If the paper is found to have scholarly weaknesses, the author may be asked to make improvements; or if it is just not up to standards, it may be rejected. While this isn't a perfect process, it does mean that works appearing in scholarly publications are more likely to be credible and reliable and thus good sources for your research.

In addition to academic journals, other publications produced by scholarly or professional societies will use some kind of peer review and are thus good places to look for credible sources. Publications from major universities or other institutions of higher learning also tend to be more reliable. Major book publishing houses can also be a good source for reliable, credible sources as long as they are known for producing scholarly work as opposed to popular books that are aimed at a general readership. Publishers that have an academic imprint will generally produce reliable materials. Some reputable think tanks will also produce good material. There isn't an exact science to finding reliable printed materials, but over time, as you work within a particular field, you will learn which publishers you can count on for the best sources.

While finding good sources isn't an exact science, there are certain sources of information that you should almost always avoid in your search for credible, authoritative information that can support a good argument. Magazines, for instance, should almost always be thought of as entertainment rather than as a source of authoritative information on any particular topic. It cannot be emphasized enough that magazine publishers make decisions about what to print based almost exclusively on what they think will sell more copies of the magazine. Therefore, the editorial boards work hard to make sure that they print material their audience already agrees with—whether it is right or wrong, good or bad, reliable or not. Even when you are reading a well-known magazine with a very good reputation, you must always remember that the article you are reading was printed so that you would buy the magazine, not because it represents the most authoritative expertise in the field. Of course it might so happen that the information *is* reliable, but in a magazine that does not use some form of peer review, there is no way to be sure. The same can be said of newspapers. While newspapers are generally good at reporting the basic facts of what happened, where, and to whom, they also contain articles that are written primarily to sell newspapers. So it is best to avoid these kinds of periodicals if you want to find credible information to support your arguments.

You must also be cautious when reading printed books. The technology required to produce printed books has advanced to the point that almost anyone can do it. Many publishing businesses cater specifically to authors who are willing to pay in advance for their books to be printed. As long as an author has a manuscript and enough money to pay the fees, the book can be produced without much effort. There was a time when self-published works were rare and hard to come by, and they were usually only available for sale by the authors themselves. But with the advances in printing technology, even major bookstores and large online retailers now sell books that authors have paid the publisher to print. Of course these books can be helpful and often contain very good information. However, since they are not subject to any kind of expert review, they are less helpful in bolstering your arguments. When looking for credible, authoritative information to provide strength to your arguments, you should consult books that are produced by major publishing houses that have a long-standing reputation for producing high-quality materials.

As with self-published works, you should also be cautious when consulting materials printed by an organization whose purpose is to advance one particular point of view on controversial topics. Of course nothing is wrong with working hard to advance one particular point of view, and these kinds of organizations often do good, scholarly work. But when you are making an argument, appealing *only* to one-sided sources can introduce bias that becomes counter-productive to the goals of the argument (convincing someone that the claim is true).[1] You can strengthen your argument by appealing to organizations known for objectivity rather than appealing to materials published by organizations known for being one-sided. Academic journals, for example, routinely publish opposing points of view; sometimes essays written by authors on opposite sides of a debate will be included in the same issue. Your arguments are stronger if you rely on these kinds of sources because it shows your audience that you are not unduly biased.

Current Information

The scholarly, credible sources you rely on should also be current. Human knowledge is fast moving, and what was cutting-edge scholarship fifty years ago may be obsolete now. Historical sources can still be quite valuable, of course; but if you are making an argument about the New Testament, you should consult the most recent New Testament scholarship. Even if you are discussing a matter of ancient

1. What makes things more difficult is that biased groups, who focus only on advancing a particular agenda, often hide their true nature and masquerade as "independent" research organizations, and it may take work on your part to discover this. It is worth your time to vet any organization to make sure it is not one-sided.

history, you should consult the most recent textual or archeological research. If you rely on an old argument as support, and that old argument has since been defeated, your argument will likely not fare any better. What information is considered current isn't the same for every issue you study. Your goal, however, should be to write arguments informed by the most recent and most reliable scholarly research available pertaining to your topic.

You also need to take care to find an author's most recent published works when you are analyzing or evaluating that author's position. Scholars sometimes modify their viewpoints or abandon old views entirely in favor of new positions on controversial issues. Admittedly, scholars tend to be a stubborn sort and rarely change their minds about anything, but they often refine their arguments and ideas. Philosopher of religion Richard Swinburne, for example, has modified his views on God's relation to time. If you quote Swinburne on this topic in his work from the 1960s, it will not reflect his final position on the topic.[2] An author's later publications will often serve to clarify earlier misunderstandings or improve upon earlier work. If you want to make an argument about a published author's point of view, it is a basic requirement for you to consult that author's most recent work. Out of respect for that scholar, you must make sure you are citing only the most refined, well-articulated version of that scholar's position. Doing so will help you create stronger arguments that are more likely to persuade your audience.

Cautions for Researching Online

Extra caution is required when you are looking for high-quality, authoritative sources in online research. Again, technology has advanced to the point that just about anyone can create a professional website and publish material there that has the appearance of high quality. As a result, many of the same criteria you look for

2. See, e.g., Richard Swinburne, "God and Time," in *Reasoned Faith: Essays in Philosophical Theology in Honor of Norman Kretzmann*, ed. Eleonore Stump (Ithaca, NY: Cornell University Press, 1993), 204–22. In the opening paragraph of the essay, Swinburne states that he intends to offer "a rebuttal of a thesis that [he] had previously defended in print" (204).

in printed sources also apply to websites: authored by recognized experts, published by major universities or other scholarly organizations, and containing current information. One key distinction you must learn to make is between a helper website and a bona fide research website. Helper websites point you in the right direction and lead you to other websites with high-quality, authoritative scholarly information. Helper websites can be search engines, generic or topic-oriented websites (like Wikipedia or Bible.org), websites specializing in question-and-answer discussions, and personal websites and blogs. These kinds of websites should not be considered the final stop when searching for credible support for your arguments. Instead, think of them as providing help in your search for higher-quality sources. If you want to analyze an argument advanced by an atheist, you should not get your information from Infidels.org—but you might find on that website references and citations to an atheist's published scholarly works. If you are making an argument about the life of Jesus, you probably shouldn't cite a pastor's personal blog entry—but you might find in that blog entry a citation to a helpful scholarly book about Jesus. Understanding that the proper use of these kinds of sites is as helpers will be critical for your online research. The internet can be a powerful and extraordinarily helpful research tool; but if you want to use it to better your arguments, you must consult and cite high-quality, authoritative online sources.

Quoting and Citing in Written and Oral Arguments

Once you find an authoritative source you want to use, you must quote and cite the source properly. If you pick up any style manual (e.g., Turabian, *The Chicago Manual of Style*, an MLA handbook), you will find good information on formatting and other mechanics of citing and quoting your sources. We don't want to repeat that same information here because those manuals do it well. Instead, we'd like to (briefly) focus your attention on the bigger picture of how to use your sources properly, so we offer just a few bits of advice.

First, always make it clear to your audience when you are depending on another author's words or ideas in developing your own arguments. Most style manuals give you particular formatting requirements for referencing and citing another's argument in written form. When it comes to quoting sources, citing them in footnotes, and listing them in a bibliography, however, it isn't simply a matter of following formal rules for formatting. It is also a matter of integrity: in order to give proper credit to the authors whose words and ideas you are depending on, it is absolutely essential that you provide your reader with all of the required and expected information. That means that *any time* you rely on another's arguments or ideas, you must name that person and tell your audience explicitly that you are using that person's words or ideas.

Second, give your audience enough information that they can find the same sources you used. If you present an argument in written form and you relied on another scholar's work, you need to make sure your readers have all the details they need to find the exact source you found and to look at it on their own. The bare minimum information required is this: the author's full name, the title of the work, the revision or edition number (if there is one), the page number you are citing from, and the year of publication. Most style manuals also require the name of the publisher and the location of publication. When citing electronic books, you must provide "stable" location information connected to chapters, headings, and subheadings—things that don't change based on whether it is electronic or in print. The point of this is that you want your reader to be able to easily locate the exact source and the exact place in the source you are citing.

Third, don't cut corners when delivering arguments orally. When you speak (such as in a sermon, a public speech, or a presentation before a large group), you may be tempted to omit important details when it comes to citing your sources. In written form, you know you can't get away with an incomplete footnote or with omitting the title of a work you consulted. When speaking in public, you might think you can omit essential information about your sources and no one will be the wiser. But remember that arguments are aimed at those with whom you disagree, and that audience may press you for those details or be suspicious of you if you don't provide them. You can head off any of those suspicions by stating all the necessary details: name the author you consulted, the title of the work, and the year it was published. Keep those details (along with details about where you found it) in your written notes so that if someone asks you, you can readily supply them.

Related to that, remember that when you deliver an argument orally, your audience doesn't have important visual cues that can help them understand what you are doing. In a written argument, the presence of a footnote number at the end of a sentence, the footnote at the bottom of the page, and quotation marks around words or phrases all serve to help your reader understand that you are using another author's ideas and how you are using them. When you are speaking, your audience doesn't have these helpful indicators, so you must take care to speak differently than you write—tell your audience what you are doing. Ensure that when you prepare your remarks, you plan to say enough that your audience knows just as much about when and how you are using another author's material as they would if they were reading your written argument. If you are accustomed only to writing arguments, you may find it awkward to say some of these details out loud, but your audience will appreciate it and will have more confidence in the information you are presenting.

Conclusion

Good sources make up a significant portion of the research process as you explore how to support your argument. If your intended audience is primarily comprised of those who disagree with you—if your goal is to convince them that your conclusions are justified—then finding high-quality sources is a vital part of your task. Citing recognized experts can go a long way toward convincing your audience that you have a good understanding of the issues pertaining to your argument, even those that lie outside your own area of expertise. Since you don't know everything, it is essential that you learn how to find and cite experts at key points in your argument. Do not take this charge lightly. Instead, invest in the research process so that you are ready and equipped to clearly articulate why you believe in the way you do—so that others might eventually believe also.

9

Making Your Case

So far we have given you bits and pieces of advice (important bits and pieces, but bits and pieces nonetheless) for making good arguments. In this final chapter we draw together some of the guiding principles and specific guidelines to give you a better idea of how to put those guidelines into practice to persuade your audience. What we have in mind is what might be called a "long form argument," such as you might find in an academic paper or essay, a speech, or perhaps a sermon. These kinds of arguments have many smaller parts, and we want to begin the process of showing you how to put it all together to make your case. We present this in the following six tips for making a case.

Tip 1: Know Your Audience and Your Purpose

By our account there are three common reasons for creating an argument. Before we mention these reasons, we want to give a couple of disclaimers. First, many students write an argument as part of an assignment for a class, but we aren't going to discuss that here. The reason for this is that the class assignment should be seen as a learning exercise, helping you to understand how to present an argument in written form. It is the training ground for one of three reasons (or others you can think of). Second, we want to note a hierarchy to the reasons we are about to mention: the second and third reasons ultimately serve the first.

The first reason to give an argument is to convince an audience to accept your particular belief when your belief conflicts with the audience's current belief on the topic. Throughout this book we have implied this as the primary context for creating a good argument, and indeed, depending on the context in which you find yourself, this may be the most common occasion that calls for you to craft a good argument. This kind of argumentation is often referred to as "apologetics." Apologetics is the task of defending a belief through well-reasoned arguments. There are many kinds of apologetic arguments. For example, Christian apologetics is the task of making arguments to defend Christian beliefs as true or reasonable as a step toward making an appeal for the non-Christian to adopt Christianity. Apologetics is not limited to defending Christian beliefs, of course. Any time an argument is presented to defend a belief or set of beliefs, in hopes that the audience will adopt those beliefs as true (or at least concede that they are rational), it is proper to call it an exercise in apologetics. When you find yourself in this situation, you will need to think about the best ways to win your audience over to your way of thinking and craft your argument accordingly.

The second reason for making an argument is to help an audience have confidence in their beliefs by supplying clear reasoning that supports those beliefs. This type of argumentation might be done from the pulpit or the lectern. Rich currently serves as copastor of a church, and giving reasons to his congregation for beliefs that they already hold is the kind of argumentation he often engages in during his preaching. Most of those in attendance are generally in agreement about the fundamentals of Christianity; even though the audience already agrees on the main beliefs that Rich presents, he argues anyway so that the audience can have confidence in knowing that their beliefs are supported by good reasoning and can be defended with good arguments. His argument is not to convince them to adopt a belief that they currently do not have, but rather to reaffirm their understanding so they can be confident in what they believe. In some similar cases, the audience might simply be unaware of how to properly support a particular belief they hold. In cases such as these, it is important to make a good argument as an example that shows the support for that belief. There are many occasions in which you might need to create an argument for similar confidence-boosting effects in your audience. This will require a slightly different style of argument from when you are defending beliefs to an audience that does not share them. Instead of focusing on persuasion, you will need to focus on demonstrating clear lines of reasoning for the purpose of instilling confidence.

The third reason for crafting an argument could be called *preparation*. What we have in mind here is presenting arguments mainly to those who are young or who are not yet familiar with the important ideas related to the topic of the argument. In these situations, arguments can be presented as a kind of introduction to the key ideas and to prepare the audience for challenges to those beliefs, which they may face at some point in the future. One common example of this might be what takes place in a church youth group, in a high school Bible class, or for children within the family unit. Young Christians, for example, are often confused about the many theological options available to them in this world. So, arguments that defend Christianity can be useful in preparing them for the various worldviews that will vie for their attention throughout life. You can think of this as predicting potential challenges that may come in the future and heading them off at the pass. It is an exercise in familiarizing your audience with challenges to their beliefs before they even realize that there are challenges, so that when they do face those challenges, they are prepared with good reasons and arguments and thus can remain confident in their beliefs and even defend them if necessary.

As mentioned above, there is a kind of hierarchy to these three reasons: the second and third reasons support the first reason. The ultimate purpose of instilling confidence in beliefs already held (the second reason) is to equip the audience to present their own arguments, so that others who do not share their beliefs may consider their claims. Similarly, the aim of preparing an audience with challenges to their beliefs about which they are not even aware (the third reason) is to equip the audience so that they can eventually engage with others about important ideas, instead of sitting safely on the sidelines of cultural engagement. Whatever your precise reason for engaging in argumentation, you must think about your overarching purpose regarding your audience, as well as your audience's perspective and whether or not they already believe your claims. Then you can craft your argument accordingly.

Tip 2: Check Your Attitude

As we have stated, good arguments are often made in order to persuade an audience that a particular belief or claim is true. But if the objective is to *persuade* an audience—convince them to jettison one belief in favor of another, for example—one of the quickest ways to derail the whole project and doom it to failure before it even begins is to adopt an arrogant attitude toward the topic. Our attitude and approach to a topic can make all the difference in the world: a good attitude will gain us a fair hearing from our audience, while a bad attitude will surely keep our audience from listening (no matter how right we are).

Unfortunately, many arguments are not offered to honestly persuade those who disagree but rather to simply gain popularity among people with whom we already agree. Unlike presenting arguments to increase the confidence of an audience who already agrees, what we have in mind here is usually an empty exercise designed to get us nothing more than pats on the back. So while there are indeed legitimate reasons to craft good arguments when our audience already believes the claim, all too often arguments are put forth as if they are targeted at those who disagree. Meanwhile, the true audience is people who already agree. Often these kinds of arguments are hostile and demeaning toward those who disagree, using unnecessarily inflammatory language, and

> If the objective is to persuade an audience—convince them to jettison one belief in favor of another, for example—one of the quickest ways to derail the whole project and doom it to failure before it even begins is to adopt an arrogant attitude toward the topic.

are delivered in a way that makes the one offering the argument appear superior to all those who may disagree. Those who offer these kinds of arguments typically adopt an attitude of unjustified confidence in their claims (at best) or outright arrogance (at worst).

> Persuasion is the art of making friends out of enemies, epistemologically speaking.

In making good arguments, it is essential to avoid this kind of approach. Persuasion is the art of making friends out of enemies, epistemologically speaking. That is, in making good arguments, we are trying to get people who disagree with us now to agree with us as a result of our argument. Consider how a fair and objective atheist might respond to the following two statements a theist might offer when delivering an argument in favor of theism. Which one do you think is most likely to cause the atheist to listen seriously, with at least some possibility of changing his mind?

1. Atheism represents intellectual foolishness. Blinded by sin, those rebels against God who deny his existence invoke weak arguments and insufficient evidence for their beliefs, and all the while they attack theists with fallacious arguments. They say that God cannot exist with evil, but this is only because they are ignorant of key philosophical issues. The argument I am about to present will show clearly and indubitably that atheism is full of obvious contradictions and cannot possibly be true, and that only ignorant people deny God's existence.

2. One of the most common objections made against theism is the problem of evil, and this is often used to justify atheism. The argument that I am about to present is intended to show that the problem of evil does not create any logical contradictions within theism, and thus is not a good reason to reject theism. My argument will further show that atheism cannot account for our ability to make moral judgments about good and evil, and thus that such a system of objective morality suggests that theism is more likely to be true than atheism.

Good arguments will be delivered with the kind of attitude represented in the second statement and will avoid the kind of attitude represented in the first. Rather than display arrogance and hostility, good arguments are delivered with an appropriate balance of confidence and humility that invites the audience—in a friendly way—to take the argument seriously and give it honest consideration.

Adopting an attitude of humility also requires that we abide by the *principle of charity*. The principle of charity is a well-known principle that governs philosophical dialogue between opponents or those who disagree about important issues. In short, the principle requires that we assume the best of our opponents: we interpret their statements and arguments in the best possible light. If it is possible to interpret our opponents' arguments as being logically fallacious or incoherent, and it is also possible to interpret those same arguments as being valid and coherent, then the principle of charity demands that we interpret them as being valid and coherent (even if we do not think that their conclusions are true). Abiding by the principle of charity will be easy for those who already take a humble approach in argumentation, but for most of us it requires some effort to avoid the temptation toward arrogance.

> The principle of charity is a well-known principle that governs philosophical dialogue between opponents or those who disagree about important issues.

Two guiding principles can serve as a reminder of why it is important for us to adopt an attitude of humility in delivering arguments. First, since we are finite and imperfect creatures, there is always the possibility that we are wrong, both in our beliefs and in the reasoning we use to support our beliefs. No matter how confident or passionate we are or how much evidence we have, the fact remains that being wrong is always a possibility. It is also possible that we made mistakes in our reasoning, even if the belief supported by that reasoning happens to be true. We are often blind to the flaws in our own thinking, so it is a serious mistake to adopt a stance of overconfidence and fail to consider our own imperfections and weaknesses.

Second, as implied in the example arguments above, it is extraordinarily difficult to persuade someone to reject their own belief and adopt yours if you belittle them, ridicule them, act superior, or say that their beliefs are obviously wrong. When treated in this manner, the common reaction is to dig in our heels and hold even more rigidly to our position. People sometimes say, "You attract more flies with honey than with vinegar." If you want to convince people to agree with you, a pleasant disposition is more suitable to the task, and arrogance is always counterproductive to your goal. Moreover, arrogance is typically paid back in kind; so also are a condescending attitude and overconfidence. If you adopt an attitude of arrogance, what starts as an argument quickly takes on the popular misunderstanding of what that term means—a verbal dispute, quarrel, or fight. Both sides draw lines, and no honest conversation is possible.

With these two principles in view, we hope you can see some real benefit to adopting an honestly humble attitude. Humility does not imply being a pushover. There is certainly nothing wrong with asserting our claims confidently—especially those that have the strongest justification, the clearest reasoning, and the most evidence. Being willing to admit that we can be wrong (and doing it honestly) is not the same thing as assuming that we probably are wrong. Confidence does not mean arrogance, and humility does not imply timidity or weakness. An attitude of humble confidence can go a long way toward earning our audience's trust and respect, enabling them to hear our good argument without being distracted by an unpleasant disposition.

Tip 3: Start and Finish with Your Claim

In chapter 1, we said that good arguments state their claims up front. An often-used saying that helps students understand how to structure a paper goes like this: first, you tell them what you are going to tell them; then you tell them; then you tell them what you told them.[1] Stated with numerous variations, the saying conveys something quite basic about how to successfully communicate: it is essential to make clear at the beginning of the presentation precisely what you aim to achieve in the presentation. The same principle applies to making arguments, whether you are presenting a rather short argument or making a larger case in a long academic paper, speech, sermon, or other presentation. In fact, the longer the presentation, the more

---

1. This particular version of the principle was used by Rich's eleventh-grade English teacher.

important it is to make clear at the very beginning the precise claim that is being made. Stating the main claim up front, at the very beginning of the argument, ensures that your audience understands what you aim to prove and can easily follow your reasoning.

Typically, the main claim is stated in an introduction—whether it is an introductory section in an academic paper or the opening remarks of a public speech. This is the "tell them what you are going to tell them" part of the presentation. Three important tasks must be accomplished in an introduction. First, you must make your audience aware of the main question under consideration. This is an identification of the topic that the presentation is about, and it also sets the context for the main claim that you intend to prove.

> Stating the main claim up front, at the very beginning of the argument, ensures that your audience understands what you aim to prove and can easily follow your reasoning.

Second, you must state the actual claim that you aim to prove (often called the *thesis* in an academic paper). Sometimes it is helpful to think of your main claim as the answer to the main question being considered. For example, if you aim to prove that God exists, then the question under consideration in your presentation is "Does God exist?" Your main claim answers that question: "Yes, God exists." Since the main claim is the most important part of the argument, it must always be stated in such a way that your audience cannot be mistaken about what you want to prove. To properly draw your audience's attention to the main claim, you can use language such as this:

- In this presentation I am going to prove that . . .
- This paper will show that . . .
- What I want you to do is reject position *A* and adopt position *B*, and I'm going to explain why you should.
- My argument is intended to demonstrate that . . .

Phrases such as these, with words such as *prove*, *show*, or *demonstrate*, help your audience understand clearly what main claim your argument is meant to prove.

Finally, the introduction section of your argument should sketch out a very brief "road map" of the main points of your argument. In telling your audience your main claim, you are showing them the destination; and in describing the contents of your argument, you are showing them how you will get there. Giving a brief preview of what premises you will offer and how those premises are connected to your main point will pay dividends in the form of your audience being able to follow along each step of the way. This will make it more likely that your audience will be persuaded by your argument.

Not only is it important to start with your main claim by crafting an introduction as we have described here, but it is also important to finish with your main claim. In an academic paper, the section in which you would revisit the main claim is usually called the *conclusion* (not to be confused with the *conclusion of your argument*, which, logically speaking, is the main claim that the argument is designed to prove, which is stated at the beginning of the presentation). If you make a presentation in oral form, the same principle applies. Just as the introduction clearly stated the main question, the main claim, and a brief sketch of how you intend to prove the claim in your presentation, so also should the conclusion accomplish these tasks. This is the "tell them what you told them" section of the presentation. The longer the presentation, the more important it is to remind your audience of the main claim you intended to prove, along with the question your claim answers and the main points of argument you presented to prove the claim. Whether your presentation is short or long, doing this at the end will result in clearer communication and thus a greater likelihood of your audience being convinced.

Tip 4: Clearly Show Your Reasoning

Once you have properly stated your claim up front, you can move on to the task of presenting the actual argument that supports the claim. When you are presenting your argument, you must clearly state the premises that support your main claim. However, it is important to do more than simply state the premises. You must also explain them thoroughly and show each element of the reasoning process that you are using so that your audience has a clear understanding of how each premise is connected to the main claim, as well as what reasoning you are using to move from the premises to the conclusion.

The structure of your presentation should follow the logical structure of the argument. Which premise comes first in your argument? State that one first in your presentation, and then devote a healthy portion of your presentation to explaining it. Then move on and do the same for the next premise. In a written argument especially, it makes sense to allow the logical structure of the argument to determine the outline of the presentation. Sometimes those who present long-form arguments (orally or in writing) are tempted to structure their presentation on the basis of the order in which they contemplated the ideas involved. When arguers do this, they adopt the "journey of discovery" method, whereby they attempt to duplicate their own process of learning and coming to their main claim in the minds of their audience. To say the least, this is an ill-advised approach that is unlikely to succeed. What is much more likely to succeed is to present your audience with the more sophisticated, refined version of your argument after you have completed your journey of discovery and put it all together in a logical structure. Allowing the structure of the argument to govern the structure of your presentation will enable your audience to see the whole argument more clearly.

> You must state the premises thoroughly and show each element of the reasoning process that you are using so that your audience has a clear understanding of how each premise is connected to the main claim, as well as what reasoning you are using to move from the premises to the conclusion.

Throughout the course of the presentation, you should strive to articulate precisely how the reasoning leads you from the premises to the conclusion of the argument. Do not rely on your audience's ability to just "see" it. Instead, take the time to explain the details of the reasoning, even those that seem fairly obvious to you. Doing this can help you avoid the charge that you have overlooked some important detail in the logic. If your argument depends on inductive reasoning, say so; and do likewise if your argument depends on deductive reasoning or a combination of both. Clearly articulating the reasoning that you use can help your audience understand exactly how the premises led you to the conclusion.

Throughout the presentation, you should also anticipate charges of fallacious reasoning and deflect them before your audience has the opportunity to make the charge. If it might appear to some in your audience that you have made an inappropriate appeal to authority, for example, you should take time in your presentation to show that your appeal to authority is not fallacious. If your reasoning depends on cause and effect, take the time to show your audience that you have not committed the *post hoc, ergo propter hoc* fallacy. If you are depending on a common form of a valid syllogism, bring that to your audience's attention, and take time to show that the form of your argument is valid. Throughout the course of the presentation, your argument will be more persuasive to your audience if you carefully demonstrate that your reasoning is valid and that you have avoided any tempting fallacies.

Tip 5: Support the Argument with Arguments

One of the best ways to defend the main claim is to anticipate and address objections your audience might have. One of the most obvious kinds of objections your audience might have concerns the truth of the main premises. The truth of your main claim depends on both the validity of the argument and the truth of the premises. Let's say that you have clearly explained your argument: you stated your claim up front, and then you explained each one of the premises used to support it. Then you explained the reasoning you used and showed how each of the premises is connected to the main claim. You showed that your reasoning is valid. Despite all of this, your audience may still reject your claim. Even if they accept your reasoning, they may reject your claim if they think that one or more of the premises you offered is false. So it is essential that you take the time in your presentation to offer any shorter arguments that may be necessary to convince your audience that each major premise in your argument is more likely true than false.

Of course if one or more premises in your argument is uncontroversial, or if your audience is already likely to believe that it is true, there is no need to do this. Rather, you should devote your energy to defending the truth of any controversial premises or those that your audience will have a harder time believing. There is no exact science to deciding when you need to do this and when you don't. Doing this successfully will require that you understand the general perspective of those in your audience so that you can anticipate which premises they might want to reject. In any case, once you identify a premise that your audience might reject, it is time to craft an argument to support that premise. When you do that, you will devote a section of your presentation to that premise; in that section the premise will become the main claim, and you will offer a shorter argument for that claim. To do this, of course, you would follow all the steps you follow for any argument. You can then incorporate that shorter argument into your main presentation.

> One of the best ways to defend the main claim is to anticipate and address objections your audience might have.

Besides doubting the truth of the premises, your audience might also object to other aspects of your argument. You should work hard to anticipate objections related to the way you have defined your terms, for example. If you are creating a new term or using a controversial definition, you might need to offer a short argument that defends your use of the term. If you are drawing an analogy that your audience might think spurious, you may need to create an argument that defends your analogy and the way you are using it. If your argument depends on a questionable causal principle, you may need to stop and prove that there really is a cause-and-effect relationship. Before you finalize your presentation, you will need to carefully analyze your argument so that you can find these various aspects of your presentation that might cause your audience to object.

In addition to anticipating objections to features of your own argument, you should also do your best to anticipate your audience's objections that might be based on challenges or alternative points of view published by others. It is likely that if you are presenting an argument, regardless of the topic, others will have already presented or published arguments that contradict yours. It is also likely that if your audience is interested in the topic, they will be aware of these contradicting positions. You should be aware of these also and incorporate into your presentation some good analysis (and rebuttals) of these alternative perspectives. Create arguments that show weaknesses in aspects of your opponents' arguments, where premises are not well supported, or where there are other significant flaws. Not only will your careful analysis contribute to your overall argument; it will also increase the confidence that your audience places in your analysis because they will know you have done your homework.

Tip 6: Explain the Benefits for the Audience

In addition to anticipating and responding to your audience's objections, you should do your best to show to your audience the *benefits* of adopting your main claim. Focus primarily on the rational benefits: why the new belief you are offering helps make sense of the audience's other beliefs and creates a more coherent system of thought. If you are attempting to prove that God exists, for example, you should do your best to show that theism on the whole comports well with other important beliefs that the atheist already has. If you are making an argument in favor of a controversial public policy your audience resists or rejects, you should strive to show how the policy is consistent with other policies that your audience accepts or desires. If you are urging your audience to adopt a particular theological position, you should show that the position makes their own theological system more coherent or complete. All of these show rational benefits to your point of view and will go a long way in helping the audience to adopt the claim you are making.

> In addition to anticipating and responding to your audience's objections, you should do your best to show to your audience the benefits of adopting your main claim.

In addition to showing the rational benefits of your main claim, you may also want to mention some potential personal benefits that may come to your listeners if they adopt your point of view. If the policy position you are advocating is the right position and will also save money for your audience, then you should include that in your description of the benefits. The fact that it will save money may not be the reason that the position is right, but it will appeal to your audience nonetheless. If the course of action you are advocating preserves valuable resources, reduces interpersonal conflict, makes future actions easier, or otherwise benefits your audience, you should mention this—even if these factors do not have a direct rational connection to whether your position is right or true. As long as you make it clear that you are not saying your position is right *because it has these benefits*, you are not committing a fallacy, and it is perfectly appropriate to include discussion of these benefits in your presentation as part of your appeal to your audience.

> Arguments are important because we have a message we believe is related to life and death, and because of this belief we have something that needs to be said and heard.

Concluding Thoughts

For Christians, good arguments are important. They are important as we argue within our churches; they are important as we present arguments in the public square and in our youth groups; and they are important as we present research and argue for truth in the halls of the academy. Ultimately, they are important because we have a message we believe is related to life and death, and because of this belief we have something that needs to be said and heard. The means, mannerisms, and methods by which we choose to communicate this message are foundationally important. Too often Christians have been content with simplistic approaches for expressing the message we have. Easy believism is not sufficient, provocative confrontationalism is not effective, and fearful passivity is not helpful. Instead, we need to be well reasoned in our own understanding so that we can be well reasoned in our explanation and articulation of this message. It is our charge to you the reader, and to Christians everywhere, to hone your skills of argumentation so that you may be effective in presenting your commissioned message to the world.

CASE STUDIES

The following case studies are meant to be used in classroom discussion. Our goal in offering these is to highlight various principles for arguing developed throughout the book. In some cases there are specific answers. In others there may be differing analyses available as readers identify strengths and weaknesses in the arguments presented.

Case 1. On a recent car trip, Ben's children were in the backseat watching the 2012 Universal Studios version of *The Lorax*, a Dr. Seuss remake. Ben wasn't paying much attention to the movie until his four-year-old daughter started singing along to it. The song she sang went like this:

> How ba-a-a-ad can I be?
> I'm just doing what comes naturally. . . .
> I'm just following my destiny.[1]

What is the implicit argument in this song? State the premises and the conclusion, and be sure to include any implied premises or claims.

Case 2. In the song "Memoir" by Audio Adrenaline, one lyric reads:

1. "How Bad Can I Be?," featured in *The Lorax*, performed by Ed Helms, voice of the Once-ler.

> I don't need theology
> to know that God's good to me.
> He's given me a family . . .

Where does the argument in these lines go awry? Break down the premises and the conclusion.

Case 3. Galatians 3:16–18 states:

> Now the promises were made to Abraham and to his offspring. It does not say, "And to offsprings," referring to many, but referring to one, "And to your offspring," who is Christ. This is what I mean: the law, which came 430 years afterward, does not annul a covenant previously ratified by God, so as to make the promise void. For if the inheritance comes by the law, it no longer comes by promise; but God gave it to Abraham by a promise.

Galatians 3:16–18 is part of Paul's argument about the law's role in the life of believers. Identify Paul's premises in this portion of his argument.

Case 4. A Bible study leader makes the following argument:

> Moses fasted for forty days when receiving the commandments in the wilderness (Exod. 34).
> Elijah fasted for forty days after fleeing from Jezebel (1 Kings 19).
> Jesus fasted for forty days in the wilderness (Matt. 4).
> Therefore, all Christians should plan to fast for forty days (potentially in the wilderness).

What kind of argument is this? What are the strengths and weaknesses of the argument? Can it be improved? If so, how?

Case 5. A pro-life proponent makes the following argument:

> God has given life to all created people.
> An unborn baby is a created person.
> Therefore, God is pro-life.

A pro-choice proponent responds:

> God gives a measure of freedom to humanity.
> The measure of freedom given by God allows us to make choices in life.
> Therefore, God is pro-choice.

Which of these arguments is valid? Why? How effective are these arguments for their opposite conclusions? Why are they or aren't they effective? Try to develop better arguments than these.

Case 6. During the 2016 election cycle, Sen. Elizabeth Warren, campaigning on behalf of Hillary Clinton, declared: "Donald Trump says he'll 'Make America Great Again.' . . . 'It's right there. It's stamped on the front of his goofy hat. You wanna see goofy? Look at him in that hat.'" Trump later responded to Warren's argument by stating of Warren: "She made up her heritage, which I think is racist. I think she's a racist actually because what she did was very racist."[2]

Are one or both of these arguments an example of an *ad hominem* attack? Explain why or why not. What would need to be added or taken away from either of them to make them examples of the *ad hominem* fallacy?

Case 7. A picture recently circulated on Facebook featuring a man holding a sign that read, "Gun sellers are accomplices of crimes." Next to this individual was a man holding a sign that read, "Spoons made me fat."

Is the second man's rejoinder a fair argument from analogy, or does it stretch the analogy too far? Why or why not?

Case 8. William Paley argued for God's existence using the teleological argument for God's existence. This watchmaker argument is

2. Cody Derespina, "Trump, Clinton Surrogates Brawl as Race Heats Up," *Fox News*, June 27, 2016, http://www.foxnews.com/politics/2016/06/27/trump-clinton-surrogates-brawl-as-race-heats-up.html.

essentially an argument from design that supposes that when we see a watch, we know that somewhere there is a watchmaker. We recognize design-like features in the watch and conclude that it had a designer or maker. By analogy, when we recognize design-like features in the physical world, we conclude that it also has a designer or maker. Said another way by Anthony Weston,

> Beautiful and well-built houses must have "makers": designers and builders.
>
> The world is *like* a beautiful and well-built house.
>
> Therefore, the world also must have a "maker": a Designer and Builder, God.

Weston critiques this argument by analogy, saying,

> Whether the world really *is* relevantly similar to a house, though, is not so clear. We know quite a bit about the causes of houses. But houses are *parts* of the world. We know very little, actually, about the structure of the world (the universe) as a *whole* or about what sorts of causes it might be expected to have. The philosopher David Hume discussed this argument in his *Dialogues Concerning Natural Religion* and asked:
>
>> Is part of nature a rule for the whole? . . . Think [of how] wide a step you have taken when you compared houses . . . to the universe, and from their similarity in some circumstances inferred a similarity in their causes. . . . Does not the great disproportion bar all comparison and inference?
>
> Hume therefore suggests that the universe is *not* relevantly similar to a house. Houses indeed imply "makers" beyond themselves, but for all we know the universe as a whole may contain its cause within itself, or perhaps has some kind of causes unique to universes. This analogy, then, makes a poor argument. Some other kind of argument is probably needed if the existence of God is to be inferred from the nature of the world.[3]

3. Anthony Weston, *A Rulebook for Arguments*, 4th ed. (Indianapolis: Hackett, 2009), 22. In this quote Weston cites David Hume, *Dialogues Concerning Natural Religion* (1779; repr., Indianapolis: Hackett, 1980), 19.

Critique the basic argument by Paley and then critique the rebuttal by Weston and Hume. Is the conclusion of the watchmaker analogy too far from its relative premises to be a valid argument for God's existence? Does this argument from design sufficiently meet the expectations of a substantive argument by analogy? Could/should the analogy be improved to strengthen its appeal?

Case 9. In his first proof for the existence of God in his cosmological argument, Thomas Aquinas writes,

> The first and more manifest way is the argument from motion. It is certain, and evident to our senses, that in the world some things are in motion. Now whatever is in motion is put in motion by another, for nothing can be in motion except it is in potentiality to that towards which it is in motion; whereas a thing moves inasmuch as it is an act. For motion is nothing else than the reduction of something from potentiality to actuality. But nothing can be reduced from potentiality to actuality, except by something in a state of actuality. Thus that which is actually hot, as fire, makes wood, which is potentially hot, to be actually hot, and thereby moves and changes it. Now it is not possible that the same thing should be at once in actuality and potentiality in the same respect, but only in different respects. For what is actually hot cannot simultaneously be potentially hot; but it is simultaneously potentially cold. It is therefore impossible that in the same respect and in the same way a thing should be both mover and moved, i.e., that it should move itself. Therefore, whatever is in motion must be put in motion by another. If that by which it is put in motion be itself put in motion, then this also must needs be put in motion by another, and that by another again. But this cannot go on to infinity, because then there would be no first mover, and, consequently, no other mover; seeing that subsequent movers move only inasmuch as they are put in motion by the first mover; as the staff moves only because it is put in motion by the hand. Therefore it is necessary to arrive at a first mover, put in motion by no other; and this everyone understands to be God.[4]

Identify the various causes and effects in Aquinas's argument.

4. Thomas Aquinas, "The Existence of God," in *The Summa Theologica of St. Thomas Aquinas*, trans. The Fathers of the English Dominican Province, vol. 1 (1920; repr., New York: Benziger Brothers, 1947), 13.

Case 10. In Aquinas's second argument for the existence of God, he starts with the nature of the efficient cause:

> In the world of sense we find there is an order of efficient causes. There is no case known (neither is it, indeed, possible) in which a thing is found to be the efficient cause of itself; for so it would be prior to itself, which is impossible. Now in efficient causes it is not possible to go on to infinity, because in all efficient causes following in order, the first is the cause of the intermediate cause, and the intermediate is the cause of the ultimate cause, whether the intermediate cause be several, or one only. Now to take away the cause is to take away the effect. Therefore, if there be no first cause among efficient causes, there will be no ultimate, nor any intermediate cause. But if in efficient causes it is possible to go on to infinity, there will be no first efficient cause, neither will there be an ultimate effect, nor any intermediate efficient causes; all of which is plainly false. Therefore it is necessary to admit a first efficient cause, to which everyone gives the name of God.[5]

Evaluate Aquinas's causal reasoning. What are the strengths and weaknesses of his reasoning? Does his reasoning convince you of his conclusion? Why or why not?

Case 11. Darwin observed changes in finches on the Galapagos Islands. Based on his observations, modern scientists have expanded his research to propose various naturalistic views of the history of life.

Were Darwin's observations deductive or inductive in nature? Write out some of the premises that Darwin (and others) may have relied on to reach their conclusions, and then identify how these premises are connected to the conclusion.

Case 12. A new student was assigned to write a research paper on justification. After some cursory research and using a handy Merriam-Webster's dictionary, the student introduced the paper by saying:

> If you have been paying attention to anything theological over the past decade, you have heard the name N. T. Wright and his proposals related to the New Perspective of Paul. Wright is a theologian of the

5. Ibid.

Church of England. He was bishop of Durham until 2010 and then took a professorship at the University of St. Andrews, where he is professor of New Testament and early Christianity. His writings are prolific and the reception is varied. Some praise his insight as a new theological reformation, and others castigate it as recycled heresy. The essence of the debate surrounding his theology centers on his views regarding the doctrine of justification. John Piper, a Reformed pastor and prolific author, is also quite interested in writing on the doctrine of justification. He too has a passion for this topic and a desire to explore the biblical themes surrounding justification. In one of his books, he engages Wright's ideas, leading one reviewer to conclude, "By writing this book he has done us all, including N. T. Wright, a great favor."[6] Thus, the following essay will harmonize the theologies of justification from these two eminent theologians.

What is the major problem with this introduction and the argument the student is implying for the direction of the paper? What would be needed to improve this argument for the sake of an audience's understanding?

Case 13. Luke 14:1–6 says:

One Sabbath, when he went to dine at the house of a ruler of the Pharisees, they were watching him carefully. And behold, there was a man before him who had dropsy. And Jesus responded to the lawyers and Pharisees, saying, "Is it lawful to heal on the Sabbath, or not?" But they remained silent. Then he took him and healed him and sent him away. And he said to them, "Which of you, having a son or an ox that has fallen into a well on a Sabbath day, will not immediately pull him out?" And they could not reply to these things.

What type of argument is Jesus making in this passage? Identify the various components of his argument and offer an analysis on his implied conclusion.

Case 14. In 1 Timothy 5:18, Paul makes a very simple but pointed statement: "You shall not muzzle an ox."

6. Richard B. Gaffin, back cover endorsement for John Piper's *The Future of Justification: A Response to N. T. Wright* (Wheaton: Crossway, 2007).

In the larger context of this verse, what type of argument is Paul making? What is the point of his argument? How effective is this argument in accomplishing his communicative goals?

Case 15. In a commentary on Malachi, Pieter A. Verhoef comments on the date of this book, saying, "Although we do not have any direct indication of Malachi's date, neither in Scripture nor in tradition, we may deduce from indirect evidence the approximate date of the prophecy."[7] Verhoef then presents his own reasons for preferring to date Malachi between 445 and 433 BC.

Is this argument deductive or inductive? Why?

Case 16. Disagreeing with Verhoef's argument (in case 15), Andrew E. Hill uses linguistic commonalities in his dating of Malachi. He writes,

> Careful study of the Hebrew language of Malachi . . . reveals that the book has considerable linguistic similarities with Old Testament writings dated to the sixth rather than the fifth century BC. Based on the detailed information gleaned from this kind of technical linguistic analysis of the postexilic prophets, we conclude that Malachi was most likely composed in Jerusalem during the very early years of religious and social decline prior to the time of Ezra the scribe (roughly 500 to 475 BC).[8]

What type of argument would Hill use to present his case favoring this date of Malachi? Is this the type of argument that can be stronger and weaker? If so, how could he strengthen his argument?

Case 17. A pastor quotes these verses: "In the beginning was the Word, and the Word was with God, and the Word was God. He was in the beginning with God. All things were made through him, and without him was not any thing made that was made" (John 1:1–3). Based on this passage, he argues that it is readily evident that the Word of God is inerrant, since the Word was with God from the beginning.

---

7. Pieter A. Verhoef, *The Books of Haggai and Malachi*, New International Commentary on the Old Testament (Grand Rapids: Eerdmans, 1987), 156.
8. Andrew E. Hill and John H. Walton, *A Survey of the Old Testament*, 3rd ed. (Grand Rapids: Zondervan, 2009), 704.

Which fallacy best identifies the poor argumentation in this case for biblical authority?

Case 18. In his book on the truthfulness of the Christian Scriptures, John Piper begins a chapter with the following introduction:

> My concern . . . has been to find a way to have a well-grounded confidence in the truth of the Bible based on evidence that a person can see, even if he has no historical training and little time to devote to rigorous study. . . .
>
> One way to think about this approach is to compare it to the confidence I have that my wife is faithful to me—that she is not having an affair with another man. How can I have a well-grounded confidence that she is faithful? One approach would be to hire a private detective and assign him to do the necessary surveillance to prove she is not having a secret rendezvous. But that approach leaves me worried that the private detective may not be thorough. Maybe he missed something. Maybe she suspects he is there and has found a way to send him on a wild-goose chase while she carries on her affair. This approach is going to leave me worried and unconvinced.
>
> The only way to have the kind of well-grounded confidence in my wife that leaves me with complete peace of mind is to base it on a direct awareness of the kind of person she is. Over time I come to know her very deeply. I see the profound marks of integrity and holiness and the fear of God and devotion to Christ and to me. These are realities that no private detective can prove to me. I know them firsthand. I cannot quantify them. If I could, they would lose their force, because then I would always be wondering if I need a little more "quantity" to establish her character. It's not like that. It is more immediate. More intuitive. But not merely subjective. It is based on countless hours and experiences together. This way of knowing the faithfulness of my wife produces a well-grounded confidence that I would stake my life on. I sleep peacefully without fretting.
>
> If this is possible in the case of a wife who is merely human and is imperfect and sinful, how much more is it possible to know in a direct way the truth and faithfulness of God's word, as the divine glory of his character appears through the Scriptures he inspired. In this chapter, I want to pursue this way of knowing the truth of Scripture by relating it to Pascal's Wager. The reason I think this will shed more light on how we gain a well-grounded confidence in Scripture is that the

inadequacy of Pascal's Wager sends us to the Scriptures themselves with insights that deepen and strengthen our understanding of how we know the Bible is true.[9]

Piper is introducing an argument for the truthfulness of Christian Scripture. What kind of argument is he using here? In your estimation, how effective is this approach for arguing for the reliability of Christian Scripture?

Case 19. In an article in *The New Yorker*, Adam Gopnik writes:

> Would it be possible to be an absolutist on abortion without a private metaphysical intuition, some "faith"? The strongest reasoned pro-life argument might be that human life is so unimaginably precious, and so easy to treat with indifference or contempt, that anything that interferes with it or cheapens its value is wrong. But many other views fall logically and inevitably from this one. One would have to oppose capital punishment—which is not only contemptuous of human life but has often demonstrably been performed in error. One would find it difficult to support any war or military action at all. Many other views would necessarily flow from this view, truly held; in their absence, one must doubt its authenticity, and suspect it of being a dogma dressed up as an argument.[10]

Assess the strength of Gopnik's argument and consider whether or not the relationships between these types of pro-life positions are justifiably similar for the author's conclusion to be accepted.

Case 20. In the article cited in case 19, Adam Gopnik challenges "the moral intuition that abortion is in any way like murder" by examining the behavior of those who claim to hold this intuition. Gopnik argues that such people do not actually treat abortions and homicides the same way since "only the tiniest fringe" argues that penalties for abortion should be on par with the penalties for homicide. To Gopnik, this disparity of treatment shows that most pro-life

9. John Piper, *A Peculiar Glory: How the Christian Scriptures Reveal Their Complete Truthfulness* (Wheaton: Crossway, 2016), 167–68.

10. Adam Gopnik, "Arguing Abortion," *New Yorker*, November 28, 2014, http://www.newyorker.com/news/daily-comment/arguing-abortion.

advocates do not actually believe that abortion and murder are the same. Instead he claims that arguments against abortion are based on the slippery slope fallacy: that allowing abortions will eventually lead to legalizing infanticide.[11]

Evaluate Gopnik's claim that those on the pro-life side of the abortion debate cannot argue that abortion is murder unless they also argue that abortionists and murderers should face the same legal consequences.

11. Ibid.

GLOSSARY

ad hominem. An informal fallacy committed when an argument is directed at a person instead of at a line of reasoning, in an effort to show that the opponent's conclusions are incorrect.

ad populum. An informal fallacy in which a belief is said to be true because that belief is popular.

affirming the consequent. A formal fallacy that mistakes the form of a *modus ponens* and uses the following fallacious structure:

> If A, then B.
>
> B.
>
> Therefore, A.

analogy. Comparison between two different items that draws on a relevant feature of one item to better understand the other for the purpose of clarification or explanation.

appeal to authority. Relying on expert opinion in an argument. This can be perfectly appropriate and a reliable way to determine whether certain claims are true or false. However, the fact that a person is an authority figure may be irrelevant to the claim under consideration. In such cases the appeal to authority is inappropriate and fallacious.

argument. The process of giving a systematic account of reasons in support of a claim or belief. Arguments present objective, factual claims for the purpose of persuading others to acknowledge certain facts about the world.

argument by analogy. An argument that uses the observed similarities between the items being compared as the basis for concluding that the items probably have further, unobserved similarities.

begging the question. An informal fallacy of circular reasoning in which the truth of one or more premises in an argument depends on the truth of the conclusion.

belief. A reflection on some feature of the world that one takes to be true. This can be expressed as a claim. In an argument, the conclusion or main claim being offered represents a belief of the arguer.

causal reasoning. A kind of reasoning needed to analyze the relationship between cause and effect.

cause and effect. A form of argument that (a) finds the cause of an outcome or (b) predicts the effect that will follow a cause.

circular definition. A definition that does not really explain the meaning of the word. One of the hallmarks of a circular definition is that it uses the word it seeks to define in the definition given.

claim. A statement, conclusion, or belief being defended or supported by the premises in an argument.

conclusion. The claim or belief that is defended or supported by the premises in an argument.

correlation. When two events are regularly associated with one another. Inductive reasoning can be used, moving from observed patterns of correlations to generalized conclusions about those patterns.

deductive argument. An argument in which if the premises are true, the conclusion is certainly true. All the information in the conclusion of a deductive argument is contained in the premises.

denying the antecedent. A formal fallacy that mistakes the form of a *modus tollens* and uses the following fallacious structure:

> If A, then B.
> Not A.
> Therefore, not B.

epistemology. The study of knowledge.

equivocation. An informal fallacy that improperly leverages words that have multiple meanings. This fallacy occurs when one is intentionally ambiguous in one's use of a word, so that one can apply it later in the argument with a different meaning from the first.

fallacy. In logic, a mistake in reasoning, typically because the premises do not have the proper logical relationship to the conclusion.

false dilemma. An informal fallacy that inappropriately suggests that a question has only two possible answers and that a choice must be made between those two, when in actuality more than two possible answers are available.

formal fallacy. A mistake in reasoning related to the form or structure of an argument. It is called *formal* because the defect is in the form of the argument.

genetic fallacy. An informal fallacy attempting to prove false (or true) an idea based on the source of that idea.

"if . . . then" deductive syllogism. A form of deductive argument. The two most common are *modus ponens* and *modus tollens*.

inductive argument. An argument that relies on the accumulation of evidence leading to a probable conclusion, leaving room for doubt as to whether the conclusion is true. Even if the premises are all true, the conclusion is still not certain. In inductive arguments the conclusion contains information not contained in the premises.

informal fallacy. A mistake in reasoning related to the content or the meaning of words and phrases in the argument itself.

knowledge. A belief that is held for good reasons and is true. This is often described as "justified true belief."

law of the excluded middle. An assertion that either *P* or not-*P* (but not both) must be true. That is, for any proposition, either that proposition is true or its negation is true. This principle is called *excluded middle* because it recognizes the common-sense idea that there is no middle ground between a proposition and its denial. There simply isn't anything between *P* and not-*P*.

law of identity. An assertion that whatever something is, that is what it is; $A = A$.

law of noncontradiction. An assertion that for any object x and any property F, x cannot be both F and not-F at the same time and in the same sense.

metaphor. A figure of speech comparing two objects or ideas that is useful for drawing an analogy. As opposed to a simile, the comparison is made without an explicit explanation.

modus ponens ("mode of affirming," often abbreviated MP). A form of argument that affirms a condition (A) that would guarantee the conclusion (B). Stated differently, it begins by saying that if A is true, then B is true; then it affirms that A is true, concluding, therefore, that B is also true.

modus tollens ("mode of denying," often abbreviated MT). A form of argument that seeks to deny the content in the conclusion by way of denying a condition that would guarantee the conclusion. Stated differently, MT begins the same way as MP by saying that if A is true, then B is also true; but then it denies that B is true, which leads to the conclusion that A must not be true.

objective claim. A claim that can be proven true or false because it pertains to matters of the external world.

post hoc, ergo propter hoc. Latin for "after this, therefore because of this." A fallacy based on a mistaken assumption that simply because the second event comes after the first event, the first event caused the second event.

premise. A declarative statement that conveys some meaningful fact supporting the conclusion of an argument. Good premises are those that support the main claim of the argument and can therefore help persuade an audience that the claim is true.

principle of bivalence. A principle or law implied by the law of the excluded middle that says that for any clear, unambiguous propositional statement, that statement is either true or false.

red herring. An informal fallacy intentionally distracting the audience from relevant issues. It occurs any time a person introduces a new concept that is not immediately relevant to the argument or claim under consideration, for the purpose of distracting the audience or shifting the discussion away from an undesired result.

self-serving definition. A definition constructed in a way that ensures the success of the argument, but through semantics instead of good reasoning.

simile. A figure of speech that makes a comparison between two objects or ideas and is useful for drawing an analogy. As opposed to a metaphor, the comparison is stated explicitly.

stipulation encroachment. The action of attaching a novel definition to a word or idea that already has a widely known, established meaning.

stipulative definition. A definition given to attach a new meaning to a word, usually for the purpose of convenience in the discussion.

straw man. An informal fallacy in which one creates an intentionally weakened, distorted, or obviously false version of an opponent's argument, and then attacks that version specifically because it is easier to defeat the false argument than the real argument.

subjective claim. A claim about matters of personal preference.

thesis (of an argument). The main claim, or conclusion, that is presented in an argument.

validity. The quality of having premises that are properly connected to the main claim. A valid argument is one that does not make a mistake in reasoning.

INDEX